SILVA

MATT AND TOM OLDFIELD

ULTIMATE
FOOTBALL HEROES

SILVA

FROM THE PLAYGROUND
TO THE PITCH

DINO

Published by Dino Books,
an imprint of John Blake Publishing,
The Plaza,
535 Kings Road,
Chelsea Harbour,
London SW10 0SZ

www.johnblakepublishing.com

www.facebook.com/johnblakebooks 【f】
twitter.com/jblakebooks 【t】

First published in paperback in 2019

ISBN: 978 1 78946 112 1

British Library Cataloguing-in-Publication Data:

A catalogue record for this book is available from the British Library.

Design by www.envydesign.co.uk

Printed and bound in Great Britain by Clays Ltd, Elcograf S.p.A.

1 3 5 7 9 10 8 6 4 2

John Blake Publishing is an imprint of Bonnier Books UK
www.bonnierbooks.co.uk

For all readers,
young and old(er)

ULTIMATE
FOOTBALL HEROES

Matt Oldfield is an accomplished writer and the editor-in-chief
of football review site *Of Pitch & Page*. Tom Oldfield is a freelance
sports writer and the author of biographies on Cristiano Ronaldo,
Arsène Wenger and Rafael Nadal.

Cover illustration by Dan Leydon.
To learn more about Dan visit danleydon.com
To purchase his artwork visit etsy.com/shop/footynews
Or just follow him on Twitter @danleydon

CONTENTS

ACKNOWLEDGEMENTS

First of all, I'd like to thank John Blake Publishing – and particularly my editor James Hodgkinson – for giving me the opportunity to work on these books and for supporting me throughout. Writing stories for the next generation of football fans is both an honour and a pleasure.

I wouldn't be doing this if it wasn't for my brother Tom. I owe him so much and I'm very grateful for his belief in me as an author. I feel like Robin setting out on a solo career after a great partnership with Batman. I hope I do him (Tom, not Batman) justice with these new books.

Next up, I want to thank my friends for keeping

me sane during long hours in front of the laptop. Pang, Will, Mills, Doug, John, Charlie – the laughs and the cups of coffee are always appreciated.

I've already thanked my brother but I'm also very grateful to the rest of my family, especially Melissa, Noah and of course Mum and Dad. To my parents, I owe my biggest passions: football and books. They're a real inspiration for everything I do.

Finally, I couldn't have done this without Iona's encouragement and understanding during long, work-filled weekends. Much love to you.

CHAPTER 1

CITY'S GREATEST

22 April 2018, Etihad Stadium, Manchester
After shaking hands with the Swansea City players,
David took off his tracksuit top and got ready for
action. Jumping and shouting wasn't really his style;
instead, he walked onto the pitch with a calm, quiet
confidence.

'We're going to win today,' David thought to
himself, 'and we're going to do it in style!'

His team, Manchester City, were the new Premier
League Champions, and the players couldn't wait
to celebrate that achievement in front of a heaving
home crowd. First, they would play another ninety
minutes of fantastic football, and then they would

lift the trophy. There would be plenty for the fans to cheer about:

CITY! CITY! CITY!

There was a party atmosphere in the stadium, but David was in no mood to relax. He wanted to be on the ball as often as possible, creating moments of magic for his team. Pass and move, pass and move, pass and move – that was the new City way under their amazing manager, Pep Guardiola.

The football was fast and flowing; a joy to watch and even greater joy to play. Kevin De Bruyne slid the ball through to Raheem Sterling, who pulled it back to David. The pass was slightly behind him, but he didn't panic. No, David just flicked the ball up and then volleyed it past the goalkeeper. *1–0!*

Goooooooooooooooooooooooooooooaaaaaaaaaaaaaa aaaaaaaaaalllllllllllllllllllllllllllllllllll!!!!!!!!!!!!!!!!!!!!

'Nice one, mate!' Raheem said, putting an arm around his shoulder.

The City show had started with another great team goal. David ran towards the fans with his right arm raised in the air and the thumb of his left hand in his mouth. He was dedicating the goal to his sick son, Mateo. He was always in David's thoughts, even out on the football pitch. Hopefully, Mateo would be out of the hospital soon, and then he would get to watch his dad play.

'One day!' David told himself.

After that special moment, he settled back into central midfield to play his favourite role: pass-master. That's where Pep wanted him to be, running the game for City with his remarkable touch and vision. David loved his deeper role because he had more time and space to work his magic.

'Here!' he called for the ball again and again.

David was always available, and he was always thinking one step ahead. Who should he pass to next? Could he spot anyone making a brilliant run?

Fifteen minutes in, and the Swansea players already felt like giving up. How were they supposed to win the ball back from midfield maestros like David and Kevin? They passed and passed but they never made mistakes – ever! They were just too good and soon, it was game over.

Fabian Delph to David, David back to Fabian,
Fabian across to Raheem. 2–0!

City's superstars celebrated with a big group hug.
Their Premier League title party was going exactly
according to plan.

'Nice finish!' said David.

'Nice cross!' said Raheem.

'Nice pass!' said Fabian.

In the second half, City went searching for
more. They were never satisfied, and neither were
their fans. They had come to see goals, and plenty
of them.

Kevin hit a long-range rocket. *3–0!*

David got the ball, turned beautifully and played
an unbelievable pass through to Raheem. As he went
to shoot, a defender fouled him. *Penalty!* Gabriel
Jesus missed the spot-kick, but Bernardo Silva scored
the rebound. *4–0!*

Yaya Touré chipped a ball over the top for Gabriel
to head home. *5–0!*

What a season City were having! That was their
ninety eighth goal in only thirty-five Premier League

games. They were now just five goals behind the all-time record, with four games still to go.

'We want six! We want six!' their supporters cheered merrily.

Five would do just fine, though. Job done! At the final whistle, the City players went off and then came back on wearing special shirts with '18 CHAMPIONS' on the back. One by one, they were called up to collect their winners' medals.

Number 31, Ederson...

...Number 17, Kevin De Bruyne...

...Number 10, Manchester City's all-time record goalscorer, Sergio Agüero!

The cheers got louder and louder until there were only two players left: City's two legendary leaders. Vincent Kompany, the club captain would go last, but first...

Number 21, 'El Mago', The Magician, DAVID SILVA!

When he walked up onto the stage, he waved modestly to the screaming supporters. Without a football at his feet, David didn't feel so comfortable in front of so many people. Still, he had a smile on his face as he joined his teammates. It was almost time for the big moment.

Oooooooooooooooo...

Vincent gathered everyone around him and then lifted the Premier League trophy high into the sky.

...Hurraaaaaaaaay!

It was a good thing that David never got tired of that winning feeling. He had won three major tournaments with Spain – Euro 2008, World Cup 2010 and Euro 2012 – and now seven major competitions with City – one FA Cup, three League Cups and three Premier League titles. That was a whole lot of winning and yet the celebrations were still as exciting as ever.

At last, David held the trophy in his hands. As he raised it above his head, he could hear the supporters singing:

He came from Spain with just one aim – SILVA! SILVA!

He came to make us great again, SILVA! SILVA!

When his job with us was done,

And all the trophies he had won,

We called him David Silva – CITY'S KING OF SPAIN!

Sergio scored lots of goals, Vincent was a rock at the back, but was David their greatest-ever player? The City fans certainly seemed to think so. He had changed their club forever. They had so much love and respect for 'The Magician of Arguineguín'.

CHAPTER 2

ANY BALL, ANY PITCH

'Come on, let's go out and play!' David cried out impatiently.

Like most days in Arguineguín, it was way too hot to be stuck indoors all day. The Canary Islands were part of Spain, but they were actually much nearer to the North-West coast of Africa. Although all the windows in the house were wide open, even that couldn't cool them down. It was much better to be out at the beach, with the cool ocean breeze on their faces, and a football at their feet.

'But we don't have a ball anymore,' Ranzel, his cousin, explained. 'Remember, José kicked it into the sea and the tide took it away!'

'Hey, it was a shot! If you were a better goalkeeper, maybe you'd have saved it…'

As the others argued, David tried to think of a clever plan. What else could they use instead? A stone? A bottle? A scrunched-up newspaper? Any ball would do…A-ha! He had a great idea.

'Right, you wait here and keep watch,' he told his cousins. 'If you hear Grandma coming, make lots of noise, okay?'

'Okay!'

David was the youngest of the gang, but he was also the bravest. And now that he was nearly six years old, he was allowed to go out and play a little further away than just the alley at the side of their house. As long as Ranzel was there to keep an eye on him, they could set off on fun football adventures. But first, they would need to find a new ball.

After taking a long, deep breath, David crept quietly into the kitchen and tiptoed over to the cupboards. He opened the doors slowly, so that they wouldn't make a loud creaking sound.

Phew, he was in! So, what could he see? David

knew exactly what he was looking for. It was his grandmother who had first given him the idea of playing football using fruit. She often looked after her grandchildren, while their parents were out at work. And whenever David and his cousins were making too much noise inside the house, she would throw a potato or an orange into the alley, as if they were dogs chasing a bone.

'You can play out there until you quieten down a bit,' she would tell them. 'You're driving me mad with all that shouting about football!'

So, could David find a potato in the cupboard? Or a grapefruit? Or a melon? Any ball would do... A-ha – a bag of big, juicy oranges!

'Perfect!' he smiled to himself as he took two and put one in each pocket of his shorts. They would need a back-up ball, in case the first one burst.

They knew that they weren't allowed to take anything from the kitchen cupboards, but how would their grandmother ever know? There were still plenty of oranges left.

'Let's go out and play!' David called to the

others and they followed him out onto the streets of Arguineguín.

The name meant 'quiet water' and that was a very suitable description for it. The small fishing village was a very safe and peaceful place for young kids to play. Everyone knew everyone in Arguineguín. Now that they had a ball, they just needed a football pitch. Any ball, any pitch! There wasn't much grass around, so where else could they play?

'Last one to the beach has to go in goal!' David shouted as he sprinted into the lead.

The beach was where all Canary Islanders learnt to play football. That was why they were so good at the beautiful game; almost as good as the Brazilians! It was hard work running up and down the bumpy sand, especially while kicking a ball at the same time. But luckily, David was a natural. The ball – or fruit – always stayed stuck to his foot as he glided past his cousins' tackles. He was the boy with the golden touch. Not only was he the bravest, but he was also the best at football.

'I'm on David's team!'

'No way, that's not fair. You'll thrash us!'

When they were old enough, David let his sister Natalia and his brother Nando join the football gang, but only on one condition:

'First, you've got to go get us a new "football"!'

For a long time, they thought they'd got away with their fruit-stealing tricks. They thought they were so clever, finding new 'footballs' whenever they needed them!

But then one day, David's dad gave him a special gift – a new football, made out of old cloths and rags. David's eyes grew wide with excitement. He couldn't wait to show his cousins.

'Wow, this is the best present ever. Thanks, Dad!'

Fernando laughed. 'My pleasure. At least now our kitchen cupboards will be safe!'

CHAPTER 3

SAN FERNANDO'S LITTLE WING WIZARD

On the beach in Arguineguín, David played every position all at once – defender, midfielder, right-wing, left-wing *and* striker. Sometimes, when his cousins got tired of trying and failing to tackle him, David even became a goalkeeper too. As long as he was playing football, he didn't mind where he stood on the pitch, or whether he used his hands or feet.

'You're so annoying!' Ranzel huffed as David dived across the sand to make another sensational save. 'Why do you have to be so good at everything?'

David shrugged modestly; he was just doing what he loved – playing football. Soon, however, the whole village knew about his sporting talent.

'Your son should be playing for a proper football club,' people kept telling Fernando. 'He's going to be a star!'

David was still too young to play for his local team, CD Arguineguín, but his dad decided to take him to UD San Fernando instead. It was a bigger and better football club, where David could start playing straight away.

'You're going to love it here, don't worry!' Fernando promised his son as they arrived at his first practice. 'Just enjoy yourself, okay?'

As he nodded back, David took a big gulp and opened the car door. His dad was right; there was nothing to be nervous about it. He was off to play football, and that was always fun.

At the club entrance, the San Fernando youth coach shook David's hand and then asked what he thought was a simple question:

'So, what's your favourite position, kid?'

David shrugged modestly. 'I can play anywhere,' he said. Any ball, any pitch, any position!

'That's great, but are you more of a goalscorer or a goalkeeper?'

'Both!'

At first, the youth coach was so surprised that he didn't know what to say. Most eight-year-olds were only interested in scoring goals.

'Okay, well let's start you off in goal then,' the coach decided eventually, handing him a pair of gloves. The boy was quite small for his age but perhaps he could fly through the sky like superman...

With his gloves on, David stood on his line and waited. *BANG! SAVE!* He dived down bravely to stop shot after shot.

'Excellent!' the youth coach clapped and cheered.

David got back up with a big smile on his face. Diving on a dirt pitch was a lot more painful than diving on sand but at that moment, he didn't care. He was playing football, and that was always fun.

So, had the San Fernando Under-9s found their new Number One? The coach thought so until David got the chance to use his feet instead of his hands.

FWEEEET! As soon as the match kicked off, David raced forward to challenge for the ball. He was ready to do anything to win it. Off the pitch, he was quiet and shy but, on the pitch, he was so courageous and competitive. He had his cousins to thank for that.

David kept going until the ball was his. Right, what next? In a flash, he played a quick pass to a teammate and then ran into space for the one-two.

'Pass it back!' he called for the ball confidently, as if he had been playing for the team for years.

When the first tackle arrived, David skipped straight past it with the ball stuck to his left foot. After learning to dribble on a bumpy beach, playing on a flat dirt pitch felt as easy as pie. By the time the second tackle arrived, he had slipped a clever pass through to the striker. *GOAL!*

'Excellent!' the youth coach clapped and cheered again. Wow, the kid had been telling the truth. He *could* play anywhere; he *was* good at everything.

David's goalkeeping days didn't last long. Soon,

he was San Fernando's little wing wizard, creating goal after goal with his lovely left foot.

'Your son is a very special player!' the coach told Fernando.

He smiled his best 'proud dad' smile. 'Thanks, I know!' he thought to himself.

David loved wearing the club's green shirt and starring for his team. His teammates loved playing with him too. Although he was definitely their most skilful player, he didn't show off or hog the ball. Instead, he always looked to play the perfect pass to help set up another... *GOAL!*

With David there on the wing, they knew that they couldn't lose. In no time, San Fernando were the new champions of the Canary Islands league.

Campeones, Campeones, Olé! Olé! Olé!

'We did it!' they celebrated joyfully.

What a start to his football career! David had won his first big trophy and he was still only nine years old. If he kept improving, hopefully there would be plenty more to come...

CHAPTER 4

FOOTBALL HEROES NEAR & FAR

Little David's life was already football, football, football. If he couldn't find a match to play, he would just find a match to watch instead.

'Go on, Dad!'

As soon as he was old enough, David stood on the sidelines and watched Fernando play for the local team. His dad was his first football hero.

'You can do it!'

At school and at home, David often found it hard to sit still, but it was different at football matches. He could watch quietly for the full ninety minutes – as long as he had a football at his feet! – because the action was so exciting to watch. There was so much for him to see, hear, smell and learn, both on and off the pitch. He usually returned home with lots of new tricks to try out, and, unfortunately, a few rude words as well.

'No, David!' his mum, Eva, would scold him. 'I'm serious, you can't say that – it's very naughty. Where on earth did you get that word from?'

'Football!' he would reply with a big smile on his face.

'I see. Well, I'll be speaking to your dad about that.'

When Fernando was too old to play football anymore, he started coaching football instead. That was even better because now, David had his dad standing next to him on the sidelines. They could talk tactics together and discuss the substitutions.

'What would I do without my Assistant Manager?' Fernando liked to joke.

David was still too young to be a proper coach, but he was old enough to be a ballboy during CD Arguineguín games. He loved being so close to the action, although it could be a dangerous place to be at times. One day, a man hit a powerful shot that flew wide of the goal and broke David's arm.

'Argghhhh!' he cried out in agony.

Oh dear, would that be the end of David's football career? No way! Nothing could stop him from doing what he loved most, not even a broken arm. As soon as the doctor had put a cast on it, he was back training at San Fernando again.

'Take it easy on David today!' their youth coach pleaded with his players. 'We need to have him fit for next week.'

Thanks to all the playing *and* all the watching, David was getting better and better at football. Before, it had just been a fun thing to do with friends, but now it felt more serious than that. What if, one day, he could do it as an actual job? What if he could become a professional footballer?

'We believe in you!' his family told him.

David was determined. It helped that he knew another rising star from Arguineguín. Juan Carlos Valerón was only twenty-one years old but he was already playing for Las Palmas in the Spanish Second

Division. Like David, he was an attacking midfielder with a golden touch and a killer pass. That was the Arguineguín style.

Everyone knew everyone in the little fishing village. In fact, Valerón had actually started out playing for the same local team as David's dad.

'Yeah, we played in the same team a few times,' Fernando liked to boast to his son. 'Even back then, you could tell that Juan was going to be a top player, but I helped him get there!'

So, could David go on to be 'the next Valerón'? He hoped so, but what he really, really wanted to be was 'the next Michael Laudrup'.

Laudrup was a midfield maestro who played for Real Madrid, one of the top teams in Spain. Madrid was a long way away from Arguineguín, but David watched Real play on TV whenever he could. Although many kids preferred the club's star strikers Iván Zamorano and Raúl, David chose the Dane as his number one football hero. After all, if it hadn't been for Laudrup's amazing assists, how many goals would Zamorano and Raúl have scored?

'Hardly any!' David declared passionately.

Laudrup was the perfect playmaker. He had so much speed, skill and strength. Once he got the ball, it was almost impossible to get it off him! Everyone loved watching him glide majestically across the pitch, but especially David. His eyes stayed glued to the screen to see what Laudrup would do next. Sometimes, he dribbled through defences, sometimes he played clever passes to set up the strikers, and sometimes, he also scored screamers of his own.

'Do you know what Zamorano calls him?' David argued with his friends and teammates. 'The Genius!'

It was David's dream to play football the Laudrup way, and what better place to do that than Real Madrid?

CHAPTER 5

MOVING TO MADRID?

'Your son has conquered the Canary Islands,' Vicente Miranda kept telling Fernando. 'He needs a new challenge and NOW!'

David was still only fourteen years old, but 'The Magician of Arguineguín' had already achieved so much. He was the stand-out star of the local football and *futsal* leagues, and no-one else came close to matching his talent and technique. The games were way too easy for such a promising young player. It was time for him to test himself at a higher level. David could just follow in Valerón's footsteps by joining Las Palmas, but Miranda had even bigger plans for his little protégé.

'Why don't we take him for a trial at Real Madrid?' he suggested enthusiastically.

Fernando and Eva, however, weren't so sure. Was David really ready for such a big step? Madrid, the capital city of Spain, was a long way away from the peace and quiet of island life in Arguineguín. Would their son be able to cope with that change?

'Hey, David is a lot tougher than he looks,' Miranda argued, 'and he could teach those city kids a thing or two about football!'

'Yes, you're right about that!' Fernando agreed with a smile.

As a big football fan himself, it would be a dream come true if his son went on to become a professional player. But what were the chances? Although it was clear to everyone that David had a special gift, the road ahead would be long and tricky. Lots of exceptional young footballers never made it to the top.

David's happiness was the most important thing, and football was certainly what made him happiest. His parents decided that it was worth a try, as long as it was what David wanted.

'Son, how would you feel if we took you for a trial at Real Madrid?' Fernando asked one night at dinner. 'There's no pressure at all, but Vicente thinks that it's time for you–'

David's eyes lit up immediately at the sound of those two wonderful words. 'REAL MADRID? Yes, yes, YES! When? Now?' he asked in a rush of excitement.

Eva laughed. 'Whoa, slow down for a second, Mister! It would just be for a week. Then, if it goes well, we would have to come up with a proper plan.'

'Okay cool, I'm 100 per cent in!' David nodded eagerly.

The week in Madrid was a beautiful blur. It was his first adventure away from the Canary Islands, and David loved every second of it. Everywhere he went, there was so much to see, hear, smell and learn.

'I've never seen so many people in one place!' David admitted as their taxi passed through the busy streets of Madrid.

Miranda laughed. 'Yeah, it's a bit different to

Arguineguín, isn't it? Don't worry, you'll get used to it, though!'

Despite being on trial at one of the biggest clubs in the world, David showed no fear whatsoever. Football was all about fun and winning. This was an amazing opportunity for him to play football the Laudrup way at Real Madrid – what could be better than that?

So, 'The Magician of Arguineguín' just performed his top tricks as usual. Sometimes, David dribbled through defences, sometimes he played clever passes to set up the strikers, and sometimes, he scored screamers of his own.

'Excellent work, David!' The youth coaches clapped and cheered.

'Wow, that kid is the real deal, isn't he?' they said, and Miranda just nodded.

It was all going so well; better than they had ever imagined. David even got to meet the Real Madrid manager, Vicente del Bosque. He had stopped by to watch the training session and he was very impressed.

'Well played out there, it's nice to meet a young magician in the making!' Del Bosque said, shaking his hand.

David would remember those words for the rest of his life. Another moment that he would never forget was meeting the club's star striker, Nicolas Anelka. He was too starstruck and shy to say very much, but at least he had a photo to take home and show all his friends in Arguineguín. Ranzel would be so jealous!

Before David knew it, the week was over, and he was waving goodbye to Real Madrid with a heavy heart. Oh well, hopefully, he would be back again soon and, this time, he would stay for good.

'We'll be in touch!' the youth coaches promised.

However, weeks went by and they still hadn't called. Every day, David woke up hoping for good news and every day, he went to bed feeling disappointed.

'What's taking them so long?' Fernando asked Miranda. He was just as impatient as his son. 'We can't wait around like this forever!'

'I have no idea; it doesn't make sense! The

coaches were crazy about him. Something must have happened. Let me try and find out...'

In the end, Real Madrid had decided that David was still a bit too small to join their youth academy. Miranda couldn't believe what he was hearing. Too small? The boy was still only fourteen! And what about David's silky skills – surely that was more important than his size?

'I'm so sorry,' Miranda said, trying his best to comfort his little protégé. 'I know it hurts but don't give up!'

At first, David did feel like giving up on his dream but, of course, he didn't. He loved playing football and it was what he was born to do. No, his move to Real Madrid hadn't worked out, but there were plenty of other clubs out there. And sooner or later, one of them would take a chance on his amazing potential.

CHAPTER 6

MOVING TO VALENCIA!

That club turned out to be Valencia.

Only a few months after his dream move to
Real Madrid fell through, David played in one of
Spain's biggest junior tournaments. It was another
massive chance for him to shine. There were lots of
top Spanish scouts watching, including Valencia's
Eduardo Macià.

When it came to spotting football's 'next big
thing', Macià was one of the best in the business.
With his help, Valencia had just got all the way to
the Champions League final with a team full of youth
players and smart signings. But who had they lost

to in the final? Real Madrid! David was so sick of hearing that name.

'Forget them!' he told himself. It was time to move on and find a club that really wanted him...

Valencia were a big club with big plans for the future. Macià wanted to bring in lots more promising young players. Real Madrid and Barcelona often snapped up the top Spanish talent but sometimes, they made mistakes. When they did, Valencia would be ready to pounce.

'I like the look of that kid!' Macià thought to himself.

He was watching a small winger, who was dancing across the pitch with the ball stuck to his left-foot. Just as two defenders surrounded him, the kid poked a clever pass through to the striker. *GOAL!*

BEEP! BEEP! BEEP! Macià's talent radar was going off. Why wasn't this kid already playing for Real Madrid or Barcelona?

'It's probably his height,' the Valencia scout guessed. The top clubs had decided that they didn't need more little magicians; they wanted big, tall athletes now. 'But look how brave he is – he's certainly not scared of a tackle!'

The more Macià saw, the more certain he became – he needed to invite the kid to come for a trial at Valencia.

'Another trial!' When they heard the news, David's parents were delighted, but they couldn't help feeling a little worried at the same time. What if their son got his hopes up again, only for it all to go wrong? David would be devastated if Valencia was just Real Madrid: Part Two.

But this time, everything went according to plan. The Valencia youth coaches were crazy about David and his midfield magic, and they told him straight away:

'We want to sign you for our academy!'

When he heard those wonderful words, David felt a wave of relief, joy and pride rush through his body. He had done it; he was on his way to becoming a professional footballer!

But first, he had to persuade his parents to let him go.

'Please, Mum and Dad, what if this is my only opportunity?' David begged. 'You can visit me at weekends, and I'll come back to Arguineguín for the holidays!'

'Are you sure this is what you want?' Eva asked. It was going to be hard having her young son so far away from home.

'Yes, this is what I want more than anything in the whole wide world!'

'Okay then, we better speak to Eduardo again.'

Soon, David was off on his second trip to Valencia, and this time, he was staying for good!

At first, everything was so new and exciting. David felt so independent and grown up. He was living in a dormitory with other youth players, and he was playing more football than ever. What could be better than that?

'I'm having so much fun!' he told his parents on the phone.

But as time went by, David began to miss home more and more. Valencia was a very big change, especially for a fourteen-year-old who was there on

his own. He was still living near the sea, but the
city wasn't as warm and peaceful as lovely little
Arguineguín. He wanted to go back to the quiet life,
where he knew everyone around him.

David tried to hide his feelings from his family, but
they could hear it in his voice.

'What's wrong?' his grandmother asked him. 'You
can't fool me!'

David couldn't hold it in any longer; he burst into
tears. 'Grandma, I want to come home!'

Oh dear! It didn't help that David was picking up
lots of injuries. Because he was so small and skilful,
defenders often ended up kicking his ankles as they
tried to get the ball off him.

Arghhhhh!

David never complained about the tough tackles,
but he hated not being able to play football. It was
the only reason that he was still in Valencia. Without
football, the days were so long and boring, and he
felt more homesick than ever.

'Why don't you just wear bandages on your
ankles?' one of his youth teammates suggested

helpfully. 'Then, it wouldn't hurt so much.'

But David shook his head. 'I can't because if I did that, I wouldn't be able to feel the ball properly. I need to feel it at my feet when I dribble. That would be as bad as putting a blindfold over my eyes!'

Slowly but surely, however, David found other ways to solve his problems:

How to stop homesickness? Well, his family kept him going with lots of phone calls until eventually, they decided to move to Valencia too! Fernando even got a job at the football stadium, so he could watch David play every week.

How to stop getting injured all the time? Well, by doing a little less dribbling and a little more passing, David was able to avoid a lot of the ankle kicks. That meant more game-time for Valencia's little magician to perform his tricks.

'Excellent work!' his coaches clapped and cheered after another awesome assist.

David's determination was really paying off.

Despite a difficult start at Valencia, he was now getting closer and closer to achieving his professional football dream.

CHAPTER 7

THE INTERNATIONAL ADVENTURES BEGIN!

By the time he turned seventeen, David was pushing for a place in the Valencia first-team, and he was already playing for his country.

Although the Canary Islands were a lot closer to Africa than Europe, they were part of Spain, and although David's mum was from Japan, he always thought of himself as Spanish. It was his home, his language, and his culture.

'Why would I ever play for anyone else?' he asked himself.

So, when Juan Santisteban called him up to the Spain squad for the 2003 Under-17 World Cup in Finland, David was delighted.

'Mum, Dad, I'm going to be an international footballer!' he told his parents proudly.

A World Cup? Wow, David couldn't wait to set off on his first international adventure. Who else would be joining him? He already knew Manuel Ruz, Sisi and Miguel Pallardó from the Valencia youth team, but there were lots of other, unfamiliar faces at the training camp.

'Welcome to the squad!' the captain, José Manuel Jurado, greeted him. José was a midfielder who played for Real Madrid.

'Thanks,' he replied shyly. Had they met during David's trial a few years earlier? He couldn't remember; it was all such a blur!

'Hi, I'm Cesc,' another player said, offering his hand.

'Ah, Cesc Fàbregas!' David thought to himself. He tried to play it cool, but everyone had heard of Barcelona's new wonderkid.

'Nice to meet you, I'm David.'

'Ah, David Silva!' Cesc grinned. 'Yeah, I've heard lots about you. Are you ready to win the World Cup?'

'YEAH!'

David had been given the '10' shirt, the number worn by so many amazing playmakers: Diego Maradona, Dennis Bergkamp, Zinedine Zidane, and best of all, his number one hero, Michael Laudrup. Yes, David had a lot to live up to.

For the first match of the tournament, however, Santisteban left him on the bench. Without their Number 10, Spain raced into a 2–0 lead, but just when they were cruising to victory, Sierra Leone fought back. *2–1, 2–2, 3–2!*

Spain were heading for a very embarrassing defeat. David was desperate to be the super sub who saved the day, but the manager brought on Xisco instead.

'Why am I even here if I'm not going to play?' David thought grumpily, slumping down in his seat.

For the second game against South Korea, he was on the bench again, but this time, Santisteban brought him and Cesc on at half-time. They had plenty of work to do because Spain were losing.

'Come on, let's turn this around!'

David was raring to go and ready to shine.

He scored one – *2–1!*

Then he scored a second – *2–2!*

And three minutes later, he scored a third – *3–2!*
David was Spain's hat-trick hero!

'I told you we could do it!' Cesc screamed as they
celebrated together.

It was easily the greatest moment of David's entire
life. Suddenly, everyone knew his name. Surely,
there was no way that Santisteban could drop him
after that?

He played from the start in the next match against
the USA, but for the quarter-finals against Portugal,
David was back on the bench. And he stayed there
for the semi-final against Argentina too.

Was that the end of David's tournament? It was
a very frustrating time for him, but there was good
news ahead. Spain were through to the Under-17
World Cup Final and David would be in the starting
line-up!

'I'm back!' he cheered with Cesc.

The night before the big game, David barely slept.
He was buzzing with so much nervous energy. Why

couldn't the match just kick-off now? He was ready
to shine again!

As David walked out onto the pitch in Helsinki, he
had a good feeling about the final, but unfortunately,
it ended in sadness for Spain. Brazil scored an early
goal and as hard as David, Cesc and José tried, they
just couldn't create the magic that their country
needed. At the final whistle, they sank to their knees
in despair. They had come so close to winning the
World Cup!

'Unlucky, lads, you deserved to lift that trophy,'
Santisteban comforted his tearful young players.
'You'll just have to win the Under-19 Euros next
year instead!'

September, October, November, December...
David counted down the months until the
tournament in Switzerland. But when it finally
arrived, he was the only player left from the
Under-17 World Cup squad. There was no Xisco, no
José, and no Cesc.

'Oh well, just me then!' David thought, feeling a
little lonely.

He wasn't worried, though. Spain now had so many fantastic young footballers to choose from. Sergio Ramos was a brilliant defender who played for Sevilla, and Juanfran, Borja Valero and Roberto Soldado were all José's teammates at Real Madrid.

'So, is everybody ready to win the Euros?' the captain Miquel Robusté asked as the squad arrived in Switzerland.

'YEAH!'

This time, when Spain took the lead, they held on for the victory. They won Group B by beating Germany, Turkey and Poland. The team was playing so well that David even scored a header!

'I thought that ball was going to bounce over your head, little man!' Juanfran joked afterwards.

The games got tougher in the knock-out rounds, however. After 120 minutes of football, it finished Spain 2 Ukraine 2. It was time for penalties!

'I'll go first,' David told his manager straight away, showing no fear whatsoever.

He stepped up and...scored!

'Come on!' David shouted, punching the air passionately.

Six spot-kicks later, Spain were through to the Under-19 Euro Final! There they faced Turkey, a team that they had already beaten in the group stage. David was determined to lift the trophy this time.

'It's simple,' the manager José Ufarte told them in the dressing room before the big game. 'If we work hard and play our best football, we'll win. But if we think it's just going to be a relaxing walk in the park, we'll lose!'

So, as the Spanish players lined up on the pitch for the national anthems, there wasn't a single smile in sight. Everyone was 100 per cent focused on victory.

For ninety-two minutes, however, the game remained goalless. David did his best to create chances from the left-wing, but Turkey defended brilliantly. Just when both teams were preparing for penalties, Borja twisted and turned on the edge of the penalty area and then lobbed the keeper. *1–0 to Spain!*

'What a wondergoal!' David shouted as he chased after their goalscoring hero.

Seconds later, the final whistle blew, and the real celebrations started. The Spanish players bounced up and down together in a big, happy circle. Now, there was a huge smile on every single face.

Campeones, Campeones, Olé! Olé! Olé!

What a night! David was so proud of all his teammates and their amazing achievement. They were European Champions now! During the flight home, David held on to his winners' medal carefully. It felt so good to win his first trophy for his country. Now, it was time to kick off his club career.

CHAPTER 8

LEARNING ON LOAN

David had really high hopes for the 2004–05 season. The Valencia manager Rafael Benítez had already called up several of his youth teammates to the senior squad – Raúl Albiol, Antonio Gavilán, Jaime Gavilán…So, why not one more?

'I'm ready to take the next step!' David kept telling his coaches.

They weren't so sure, however. La Liga could be a very tough learning curve for small, skilful players like David. Their little magician certainly had the talent to play at the top level, but he did he have the heart for the battle? There was only one way to find out…

'We've decided to send you out on loan,' the Valencia academy director told him. 'A full season of Second Division football will be a great experience for you. Eibar are a good club, and I'm sure they'll look after you well.'

David nodded glumly.

'Hey, it's nothing to worry about, kid. It's only for one year. Go there, do well, and you'll be back starring for Valencia in no time!'

David nodded again, and this time more cheerfully. The academy director was right; he had to think positively. This was the perfect chance to prove himself by playing week-in week-out. If he could shine at Eibar, he could shine anywhere!

'Right, so where exactly is Eibar?' David wondered.

His new club was based in the Basque Country, nearly four hundred miles north-west of Valencia. SD Eibar had been playing in the Segunda División for eighteen years in a row. But maybe David could be the hero who helped lift them up into La Liga?

'Welcome!' the Eibar manager José Luis

Mendilibar said, shaking his hand. 'We're really excited to have you here.'

David's new teammates, however, didn't look very excited to see him. Eibar's older players took one look at their new skinny, scruffy eighteen-year-old signing and thought, 'No way, this guy won't last one tackle in the Second Division!'

But it only took David a few training sessions to change their minds. He played clever passes instead of trying flashy tricks and flicks. And most importantly, he got stuck in and battled bravely for the ball. He was determined to earn his place in the Eibar starting line-up.

'Don't let those silky skills fool you,' Mendilibar laughed. 'That boy's a fighter!'

With the number '21' on the back of his red-and-blue-striped shirt, David was ready to dominate the Segunda División. Defenders tried their best to stop him by kicking his ankles, but most of the time, his feet were just too fast. Dancing in off the left wing, he created chance after chance for his new strike partner, Joseba Llorente.

'You make my life so easy!' Joseba cheered after they'd scored yet another goal together.

What a difference David was making! Suddenly, Eibar were challenging for promotion, rather than relegation. With ten games to go, the club were in third place. If they finished third, they would be playing in La Liga for the first time ever. But if they slipped down to fourth, they would be staying in the Segunda División for another season.

'Come on, we've got to keep this up!' Mendilibar urged his players.

Away at Lleida, Eibar were drawing 1–1 with seconds to go, when David dribbled through towards goal. It was an incredible opportunity for him to be the hero, but he could see that one of the defenders was down injured. What should he do?

David wanted to win, of course, but he wanted to win the right way. Sportsmanship was really important, so instead of scoring, he kicked the ball out for a throw-in.

At first, everyone in the stadium was stunned.

'Why on earth did he do that?' the Eibar fans

shouted angrily. 'He's just thrown away our best chance of promotion!'

But after the match, lots of people praised David for his fair play.

'What a brilliant role model for our young footballers!' a journalist wrote in the local newspaper.

Unfortunately, Eibar ended the season in fourth place. So close! Despite the club's highest-ever finish, they would sadly be staying in the Segunda División for another season.

But what about David? Was he heading back to Valencia to join the senior squad? He had done exactly what the academy director had asked him to do. He had shone brightly at Eibar, so brightly that Arsenal were interested in signing him. The idea of teaming up with his good friend Cesc was tempting...

'No, we want you to stay here,' the Valencia coaches told David. 'You're the future of this football club!'

The only problem was that they already had one

little magician in their team – Pablo Aimar. Was there really room for two?

'I'm sorry, we've decided to send you out on loan again,' the club told David ahead of the 2005– 06 season. 'But the good news is that this time, you'll be playing in La Liga for Celta Vigo.'

Celta were one of the three teams who had finished above Eibar in the Segunda División. Now, they were looking to survive in Spain's top league. The team had a pretty strong defence, but they were lacking some creativity in attack.

'Cool, I can add that!' David thought positively. It was time for him to show Valencia that he could light up La Liga.

After a few games on the subs bench, he slotted straight in on the Celta left-wing. He linked up beautifully with the left-back Diego Placente. It was as if they'd been playing together for years.

With ten minutes to go, Celta still hadn't scored at home to Espanyol. All their shots were either blocked by defenders or saved by the goalkeeper. Finally, a rebound fell to David. He stayed calm and slid the ball into the back of the net.

Goooooooooooooooooooooaaaaaaaaaaaaaaaaaaaaa
aaaalllllllllllllllllllllllllllllllllllllllllllll!!!!!!!!!!!!!!!!!!!!!!!!

It was his first for Celta and his first in La Liga.
What a moment! David jumped up and punched the
air with passion. 'Come on!' he screamed at the sky.

The next week, David was back to setting up
goals for the strikers. He tormented the Athletic
Bilbao right-back, shifting his body to the right, then
the left, then the right, then the left. Which way
would he go? *ZOOM!* With his quick feet flashing,
David changed direction again and dribbled into the
penalty area. He thought about shooting himself but
instead, he crossed it for an easy tap-in. *1–1!*

'Mate, that was magical!' Ángel thanked him.

Goals, assists and all-round hard work – what
a difference David was making yet again! There
was now no doubt that the little 'Magician of
Arguineguín' was brave enough to battle against the
big boys. David only missed four games all season,
and two of those were because he wasn't allowed to
play against his own club, Valencia.

'They're scared that I'll make them look silly!' he joked with his Celta teammates.

David was popular with the players and a fans' favourite too. With his help, Celta finished in sixth place in their first year back in La Liga. They were only five points behind Valencia.

'They need you back, man!' argued Ranzel, his number one fan.

David really hoped that his cousin was right. He had learnt so much on loan at Eibar and then Celta, but he had unfinished business back at Valencia. It was time to return for good.

CHAPTER 9

BACK WITH A BANG!

At last, David's wish had come true. After two successful seasons away on loan, he returned to Valencia and went straight into the starting line-up. The manager Quique Sánchez Flores had sold the team's other little magician, Pablo Aimar.

'You're our main man now!' he told David.

David loved the sound of that. And he loved being back at Valencia, playing with friends that he had known since his first days at the club as a shy little fourteen-year-old.

'Hello, stranger!' joked Raúl Albiol.

'Couldn't you just stay at Celta?' teased Jaime Gavilán. 'I'm never going to get a game now!'

No, now that he was twenty, it was time for David to shine for Valencia. After all his hard work, it was an incredible feeling to finally walk out onto the pitch, wearing his club's white shirt.

'I wasn't sure that this day would ever come,' he admitted to Ranzel.

'What? No way!' his cousin replied. 'I never doubted you for a second. You deserve this!'

David played well in his first home game at the massive Mestalla Stadium, but there was no special moment of magic. Not yet.

'Don't worry, it'll come!' Flores reassured him. 'Besides, football isn't just about goals and assists. There's all the other stuff too – the running, the tackling, the passing. You're a team player and that's so important.'

David was still finding his feet and finding his place in the team. Valencia already had Vicente, an excellent left-winger, so the manager moved David into the middle, behind their star striker, David Villa.

'Two "Davids" together,' Flores said with a smile. 'I smell danger!'

But while David Villa was scoring goal after goal, so far David Silva hadn't scored or set up a single one. That had to change and quickly.

'All I need is one,' he told Ranzel, 'and then I'll be flying!'

Away at Espanyol, Valencia were losing 1–0 with half-time approaching. Angulo chased after the ball and sent a high cross into the box. It flew just over Edu's head, but David was there behind him...

As the ball dropped down, he watched it carefully and stretched out his left leg towards it. 'Stay calm,' David told himself. He needed to get the volley just right. *BANG!*

The Espanyol goalkeeper somehow managed to block his shot, but the ball still bounced past him. It was heading towards the goal until a defender slid in and cleared it.

'Ref, that's in!' David cried out with his arm up in the air. 'The ball was over the line when he kicked it!'

The referee took a few seconds to decide but eventually, he blew his whistle and pointed to the centre circle.

*Gooooooooooooooooooooooooaaaaaaaaaaaaaaaaaa
aaaaaaaaalllllllllllllllllllllllllllllllllllllllll!!!!!!!!!!!!!!!!!!*

'Congratulations, mate!' Edu screamed as they celebrated together.

It certainly wasn't one of the best goals that David had ever scored, but that didn't matter. He was off the mark for Valencia and that was all he cared about. It was the confidence boost that he needed. Now, it was time for lift-off.

In the Champions League against Olympiakos, David curled in a beautiful cross for Fernando Morientes to head home. *GOAL!*

'What a ball that was!' Fernando thanked him. 'I couldn't miss!'

There was no stopping David now. He had found his feet and his place in the Valencia team. He raced around the pitch like he had turbo rockets hidden in his boots. He wanted to be on the ball all the time. Every touch was neat and tidy, and every pass was crafty and accurate.

'That's it – brilliant!' Flores clapped and cheered on the sidelines.

And like all top players, David seemed to save his best magic for the biggest games. When Ronaldinho's Barcelona came to the Mestalla, David was the man of the match. Early in the second-half, Angulo cut the ball back to him and he placed his shot perfectly in the bottom corner. *2-0!*

Goooooooooooooooooooooooaaaaaaaaaaaaaaaaaaa aaaaaaaaallllllllllllllllllllllllllllllllllllllll!!!!!!!!!!!!!!!!!!!

David was on fire again a few weeks later in the Champions League against Zlatan Ibrahimović's Inter Milan. With five minutes to go, Valencia were 2–1 down and on their way out of the tournament. But then a clearance dropped down towards David on the edge of the penalty area. He didn't even think about it; he trusted his technique. He ran up and struck the ball first time on the volley with his lovely left foot. It fizzed through the crowd of players and past the goalkeeper.

Goooooooooooooooooooooooaaaaaaaaaaaaaaaaaaa aaaaaaaaallllllllllllllllllllllllllllllllllllllll!!!!!!!!!!!!!!!!!!!

'You hero!' Raúl Albiol cried out, jumping up on his friend's back.

And David was at it again in the next round
against Didier Drogba's Chelsea. In the thirtieth
minute, he got to the loose ball first, dribbled
forward and *BANG!* His shot curled over Petr Čech's
outstretched arms and into the top corner.

*Goooooooooooooooooooooooaaaaaaaaaaaaaaaaa
aaaaaaaaalllllllllllllllllllllllllllllllllllllllll!!!!!!!!!!!!!!!!!!!*

It was David's best strike yet! He ran towards
the Valencia fans with his arms out wide like an
aeroplane. They were going wild for their favourite
little magician, chanting:

Silva! Silva! Silva!

As he listened, David leapt up with his fists
clenched and his heart racing. He was his team's
hero and there was no better feeling in the world. It
was what being a footballer was all about.

'Mate, what's got into you lately?' David Villa
laughed happily as they hugged. 'You're on fire!'

CHAPTER 10

SPAIN'S NEW STARS

Suddenly, everyone was admiring Valencia's little magician, including Spain's national team manager. Luis Aragonés was looking to rebuild the senior squad after their disappointing performance at the 2006 World Cup in Germany.

Raúl, their captain and top scorer, was out, and the stars of Spain's next generation were in: Andrés Iniesta, Cesc Fàbregas, Sergio Ramos...and David!

Aragonés had been keeping a close eye on him ever since the 2005 Under-20 World Cup. Cesc, Juanfran and Fernando Llorente had also played, but David was Spain's standout player. It was his best international tournament yet, even better than the Under-19 Euros.

David started by scoring a swerving free kick in the first game against Morocco and after that, his confidence was sky-high. Five minutes after coming off the bench against Chile, he won the ball, played a clever one-two, and then fired a shot into the bottom corner. He made it look so easy!

Gooooooooooooooooooooooooooaaaaaaaaaaaaaaaa aaaaaaaallllllllllllllllllllllllllllllllllll!!!!!!!!!!!!!!!!!!!!!!!!

'Nice one, mate!' Fernando cheered, giving him a high-five.

Spain were destroying Chile with their quick, one-touch passing. It was a joy to watch and an even greater joy to play. David didn't want the match to ever end.

Juanfran to Cesc, Cesc to David, David to Alberto Zapater, Alberto to Fernando. 5–0!

Cesc to Fernando, Fernando to David, David to José Enrique, José to Fernando. 6–0!

Cesc to Fernando, Fernando to José, José to David. 7–0!

'Can you pass it next time please?' Cesc asked with a smile. 'I haven't scored yet!'

'No way,' David replied cheekily. 'I'm on a hat-trick now!'

He didn't get a third goal in that game, but David did get his fourth of the tournament in the next match against Honduras. He was now only one behind their top scorer, Fernando.

'Watch out, that Golden Boot is mine!' David joked.

It was all going so well, but sadly the good times didn't last for Spain. They were knocked out in the quarter-finals by Argentina. Their talented team included Pablo Zabaleta, Sergio Agüero and the Golden Boot winner, Lionel Messi.

'That kid is incredible!' José groaned at the final whistle.

'Tell me about it!' added Cesc. He had played with Messi in the Barcelona youth team.

David was disappointed not to reach another international final, but he was pleased with his own World Cup performances. And so was Aragonés. He decided that Valencia's little magician would be perfect for his team's new quick, passing style.

A year after that Under-20 World Cup, he called David up to his squad for the first time for a friendly against Romania.

'Mum, Dad, I'm going to be a *SENIOR* international footballer!' he told his parents proudly.

'Congratulations, son!' they replied, through tears of joy.

Aragonés picked an all-Valencia front four for the game: David and Angulo on the wings, with David Villa and Fernando Morientes up front.

'Let's do this for *Los Ches!*' they cheered together before kick-off.

The Ramón de Carranza Stadium in Cádiz could only hold 16,000 supporters but David made sure that he got tickets for all of his family and friends. He didn't want any of them to miss his first senior match for Spain.

'You never know,' David said modestly, 'this could be my one and only cap.'

'Don't be silly,' Ranzel replied, shaking his head. 'You're going to get at least a hundred!'

David really hoped that his cousin was right about

that. What an honour it was to wear the famous red shirt and represent his country. The atmosphere in the stadium was amazing, with the Spain fans making as much noise as possible.

España! España! España!

Down on the pitch, their players passed and passed and passed. *Xabi Alonso to Angulo, Angulo to Cesc, Cesc to David, David to Fernando...*

The style had worked wonderfully against Chile at the Under-20 World Cup, but it wasn't so easy against Romania. Spain tried and tried, but they couldn't find a way through the defence. Although David played the full ninety minutes and helped create lots of chances, they somehow lost 1–0.

As he left the field, David was full of frustration. 'How did we let that happen?' he kept asking himself. It certainly hadn't been the dream international debut that he had imagined while growing up in Arguineguín. But had he done enough to earn a second chance?

'Unlucky,' Aragonés said, giving him a pat on the back. 'You played well tonight. Good job!'

Really? *Phew!* David was so relieved to hear that. From that match on, he became a regular in Spain's Starting XI, even if he did still wear his favourite '21' shirt. The manager switched between Andrés, Angulo and Joaquín on the right wing, but he almost always picked David on the left. Now, he just needed to start adding a few moments of magic to his solid performances...

In the Euro 2008 qualifiers against Liechtenstein, David Villa passed the ball out wide to David Silva. He looked up for the early cross, but there was no-one in the six-yard box yet. So, instead, he decided to torment the defender for a bit. He shifted his body to the right, then the left, then:

'Over here!' David Villa called out near the penalty spot, with his arms up in the air.

With his quick feet flashing, David Silva changed direction again and chipped the ball towards his teammate. David Villa jumped up and scored with a brilliant bicycle kick. *GOAL!*

'Great work both of you!' Xavi called out as he ran over to celebrate.

David now had his first international assist, but what about his first international goal? Two months later, Spain were losing 2–1 to Greece in another friendly match. Not again! He was determined to help turn things around for his team.

David Silva played a pass through to David Villa and then sprinted into the penalty area. His heart was racing. Was this his best chance yet to score? He jumped out of the way of Villa's shot, but the rebound fell at his feet. The goalkeeper saved his first attempt with his right foot, but not his second attempt with his left. *2–2!*

Goooooooooooooooooooooooooooaaaaaaaaaaaaaaaaa aaaaaaaalllllllllllllllllllllllllllllllllllllll!!!!!!!!!!!!!!!!!!!!!

'At last!' the two Davids joked together as they ran back for the restart. There was still time for Spain to win the game.

With seconds to go, Cesc dribbled forward, looking to play one last killer pass. *ZOOM!* David made a rapid run from left to right and his friend spotted it straight away. As the ball landed in front of him, David dinked it over the diving goalkeeper. *3–2 to Spain!*

Goooooooooooooooooooooooooaaaaaaaaaaaaaaaa aaaaaaaalllllllllllllllllllllllllllllllllll!!!!!!!!!!!!!!!!!!!!!!!!!

David was the hero, but he didn't forget about the man who had played the killer pass. He pointed over at Cesc and threw his arms out wide for a hug. Spain's new stars were simply unstoppable.

CHAPTER 11

THE TWO DAVIDS

As the 2007– 08 club season started, David had
one thing on his mind – trophies. His first year in
the Valencia first-team had been a big success, but
what did he have to show for it? Eight goals, three
assists and zero winners' medals. It was time to
change that.

After all, Valencia had a very strong squad, full of
top Spanish internationals: Carlos Marchena, Angulo,
Joaquín, Vicente, Fernando and, best of all, 'the Two
Davids'.

'We *have* to win something this year!' Villa said
to Silva. It was his fourth at the club, and yet he was
still empty-handed. That simply wasn't good enough.

The Two Davids started the Spanish League season like superstars in a hurry.

The Getafe goalkeeper spilled Fernando's cross straight to David Silva. *1–0!*

Fifteen minutes later, David Villa ran through and lobbed the same poor keeper. *2–0!*

Against Recreativo, Villa dribbled around the keeper instead. *1–0!*

David Silva tormented the Deportivo right-back until he just sat down and gave up! Then he curled in a perfect cross for Fernando. *4–1!*

The Real Murcia defence didn't know what to do either. They could only watch as David Silva set up David Villa to score his second of the game. *3–0!*

'You're the best!' Villa cheered, lifting the other David high into the air.

What a deadly double act! After twelve matches, Valencia were tied with Barcelona in third place, just four points behind Real Madrid.

'Let's fight for that title!' David Silva urged his teammates.

Unfortunately, however, they failed to win any

of their next nine league games. What had gone so badly wrong all of a sudden? It was a total mystery.

By January, Valencia had slipped down to eleventh place in La Liga, and they were already out of the Champions League. That meant that if The Two Davids wanted to lift a trophy, it would have to be the Spanish Cup, the 'Copa del Rey'. If they didn't win that, they wouldn't get to play in Europe at all next season. They had to do something to save their season.

'Come on, this is our last chance!'

David Silva set up one goal to beat Real Unión and then another to beat Real Betis. So far so good but things were about to get a lot tougher. In the quarter-finals, Valencia faced Atlético Madrid. They had a deadly double act of their own – Diego Forlán and Sergio Agüero.

The Valencia players knew that they had to win the first leg at home at the Mestalla. Otherwise, their trophy hunt would be over until next year...

Midway through the first half, Atlético made a mess of a clearance and the ball bounced down inside their own penalty area. Three defenders ran towards it but not quickly enough. David Silva reacted first and blasted the ball into the net.

Goooooooooooooooooooooooooooaaaaaaaaaaaaaaaa aaaaaaaalllllllllllllllllllllllllllllllllll!!!!!!!!!!!!!!!!!!!!!

'Yesssssssss!' As the crowd went wild, David clenched his fists and roared. It felt so good to score such a crucial goal for his club. That was what being a big-game player was all about.

'What a hero!' his teammates shouted as, one by one, they ran over to hug him.

Valencia held on for an important 1–0 win, and despite losing the away leg 3–2, they still went through on away goals. David's trophy dream was still alive!

Next up, however, was Barcelona. They didn't just have a deadly double act; they had a whole squad of the best footballers on the planet. Carles Puyol, Xavi, Deco, Thierry Henry, Samuel Eto'o, Messi…They were so strong that they could afford to leave Andrés on the bench!

'No, forget about them,' Raúl Albiol argued in the

Valencia dressing room. 'When we're playing at our best, we can beat anyone!'

It was true; they just had to believe in themselves. In front of 90,000 fans at the Nou Camp, they held their nerve. On the counter-attack in the second-half, David Silva slipped a clever pass through to Javier Arizmendi, who crossed to David Villa. *1–0 to Valencia!*

The Two Davids had done it again! They shared a hug as they walked back to the halfway line. 'If we keep this up, we'll be in the final!'

The first leg finished 1–1 but back at the Mestalla, Valencia stormed to a famous victory. Rubén Baraja scored a screamer and then the Two Davids each set up a goal for the team's rising star, Juan Mata. What a night for 'Los Ches'! At the final whistle, the Valencia players all joined together in a big team hug and celebrated with the fans.

'That trophy is ours!' Juan declared confidently.

First, however, they would need to beat Getafe. They might not be quite as brilliant as Barcelona, but they would still be tough opponents.

'You've done so well to get this far,' their

manager, Ronald Koeman, told them before kick-off, 'but don't let this slip now. Go out there and WIN!'

Every seat in Atlético Madrid's Vicente Calderón Stadium was sold out for the big cup final. Could Valencia win the Copa del Rey for the first time since 1999?

Yes, they could! The Two Davids started the final like superstars in a hurry. Villa played it down the left wing to Silva, who calmly picked out Juan with another fantastic cross. *1–0!*

Shortly after that, David Silva picked out Alexis with an incredible corner-kick. 2–0 and two assists already for David in the final. What a big-game player! He now had five in the competition.

'Thanks, magic man!' Alexis screamed.

'You're welcome!'

At the final whistle, David threw his arms up triumphantly. They had done it; Valencia were the 2008 Copa del Rey winners!

David couldn't wait to lift his first club trophy. As he climbed the stadium steps, he high-fived all the happy fans he passed.

'Thanks, magic man!' they cried out to him.

'You're welcome!'

3, 2, 1...Trophy Time!

As the captains Carlos and Rubén raised the cup high into the sky, David held up his own mini-trophy and sang along with his teammates.

Campeones, Campeones, Olé! Olé! Olé!

Soon, the Valencia players were parading the cup around the pitch for all the fans to see. David waited patiently for his turn to hold it. At last, he had it in his hands. He kissed it sweetly and then lifted it above his head.

Hurraaaaaaaaay!

It was a moment that David would never forget, and a feeling that he could never quite describe.

CHAPTER 12

EURO 2008

Just weeks after Valencia's Copa del Rey victory, the Two Davids, Carlos and Raúl were off to Austria and Switzerland in search of their next big trophy. Could they do their country proud at Euro 2008?

'Yes, we can!' the Spain players declared confidently.

The nation hadn't won a major tournament since 1964, but everyone agreed that this was their best chance in years. The whole football world was talking about the team's new quick, passing style.

'If you give Spain the ball, you'll never get it back!' the experts warned.

Aragonés had lots of superstars to choose from,

but he stuck with his favourites. At Euro 2008, the manager wanted to have players that he could trust to play the new Spanish way. So, the line-up was settled:

In goal: the captain Iker Casillas,

In defence: Sergio Ramos, Carlos Marchena, Carles Puyol and Joan Capdevila,

In midfield: Andrés Iniesta, Xavi, Marcos Senna and David,

And in attack: David Villa and Fernando Torres.

What a talented team! David couldn't wait to get started. He had a very good record at international tournaments – the 2003 Under-17 World Cup, the 2004 Under-19 Euros, the 2005 Under-20 World Cup – but he was playing at senior level now.

'Are you ready to win this?' Cesc asked, just like he had five years earlier in Finland.

And David's answer was still exactly the same: 'YEAH!'

Spain got off to a great start with a 4–1 riot against Russia.

First, Fernando set up David Villa for an easy tap-in. *1–0!*

Then just before half-time, David Silva raced back to intercept a pass near his own penalty area and launch a quick passing counter-attack. David to Joan, Joan to Andrés, Andrés to David Villa. *2–0!*

On the touchline, Aragonés punched the air. That was it, the new Spanish style he wanted – *pass, pass, pass, GOAL!*

And David Silva was such a key part of that plan. In their second match against Sweden, he got the ball on the edge of the box and hit a low, fizzing cross into Fernando's path. *1–0!*

David Villa wrestled Fernando to the floor and the other players piled on top of him. Spain had the talent and they had the team spirit too. For their clubs, they were rivals, but for their country, they were all united.

'Brilliant ball, mate!' Xavi called to David Silva as they jogged back for the restart.

Even when Zlatan Ibrahimović equalised for Sweden, they kept believing. In the last minute, Joan played a long ball up to David Villa and somehow, he managed to score. *2–1!*

There were emotional scenes in the stadium in Austria, and all across Spain too.

'This is our year,' the people proclaimed. 'We're going all the way!'

The Spanish players were taking it one step at a time, however. In the quarter-finals, they were up against the 2006 World Champions, Italy. When it came to knock-out football, they were the best in the business.

'Stay focused out there,' Aragonés told them. 'We can't afford to make any silly mistakes!'

Spain had to be especially careful because they were playing on 22 June. On that disastrous date, they had lost three big penalty shoot-outs in the past: against Belgium in 1986, England in 1996, and South Korea in 2002.

And in 2008, their quarter-final match went to penalties too. Spain tried and tried but they just couldn't find a way past Italy's tough defence. Even David, their danger man, couldn't create a moment of magic.

He dribbled into the box but when he pulled back his left leg to strike the ball, Daniele De Rossi slid in to block it.

Then in extra time, he finally found a bit of space, but his shot flew just wide of the post.

'Nooooo!' David groaned with his hands on his head. What a golden chance to be Spain's hero!

Instead, it was Iker who saved the day twice during the tense shoot-out. David stood on the halfway line, arm in arm with his teammates, barely able to watch the drama. At last, Cesc stepped up and scored the winning spot-kick for Spain.

Hurraaaaaaaaay!

As the ball hit the back of the net, David and his teammates were off, sprinting over to celebrate with Cesc, Iker and all the Spanish supporters. What joy and relief – they were through to the semi-finals!

España! España! España!

David and his teammates were now just two games away from winning the Euros. First up: Russia. Spain had thrashed them 4–1 in the group stage, but this time it would be a totally different match. Since then, Russia had shocked Sweden and the Netherlands. Would Spain be next?

'No way!' their players argued. As they lined up on the pitch for the national anthems, there wasn't a single smile in sight. Everyone was 100 per cent focused on victory.

Especially David. In a big game like this, Spain needed a big-game player like him. He was at the centre of everything, creating chance after chance.

He played a beautiful long pass to David Villa, who slid it through to Fernando…*Shot saved!*

He dribbled forward and found David Villa in space on the left…*Shot saved again!*

'Unlucky, keep going!' Aragonés shouted on the sidelines.

Early in the second-half, Spain finally got the goal they deserved. Andrés crossed from the left and Xavi poked it through the Russia keeper's legs. *1–0!*

'Come on!' David screamed as he jumped up on Xavi.

After that, there was only going to be one winner. Spain attacked again and again. David passed to

Cesc, who passed to Fernando... *Over the bar!*

The second goal was their best team move ever. Cesc passed to David, who played it forward to Dani Güiza, who slid it back to Sergio, who passed it into Cesc, who chipped it through to Dani, who lobbed the keeper... *2–0!*

'What a cool finish!' David cheered, hugging Dani tightly.

Dani smiled. 'I just score the goals; you pass-masters do all the hard work!'

Spain still had time for one more marvellous team move. As Andrés played it down the left wing to Cesc, David sprinted forward through the middle. He was sure that his friend would find him. When the ball arrived, he took a touch with his right foot and then placed it calmly in the bottom corner with his left. *3–0!*

Gooooooooooooooooooooooooooaaaaaaaaaaaaaaaa aaaaaaaaaallllllllllllllllllllllllllllllll!!!!!!!!!!!!!!!!!!!!!!!!

'You're the best!' David cried out as he ran into Cesc's arms. It was such an incredible feeling to score for his country at a big international tournament.

Game over – Spain were through to the Euro 2008 Final, where they would face...Germany! What a game it was going to be in Vienna's Ernst Happel Stadium.

As the two teams walked out onto the pitch, David didn't feel nervous; no, he felt as fearless as ever. He was lucky enough to be playing in a top international final. What could be better than that? Now, he just had to go out there and win it.

David worked tirelessly for his team, up and down the field, in attack *and* in defence. Aragonés knew that he could count on his little magician to fight hard for his country. He was a lot tougher than he looked.

After sixty-six minutes, David's job was done. Spain were winning 1–0, thanks to a goal from Fernando. Now, they just had to hold on for the win...

FWEEEEEEET! When the final whistle blew, David rushed off the subs bench and onto the pitch.

'We did it! We did it!' he shouted over and over again.

It would take time for their amazing achievement to really sink in. Spain were the Champions of Europe for the first time in fourty-four years!

Their captain Iker climbed up onto the balcony platform and collected the trophy. 'You ready?' he shouted to his band of brothers below. '3, 2, 1…'

Hurraaaaaaaaay!

Campeones, Campeones, Olé! Olé! Olé!

Winning the Euros with Spain was beyond David's wildest childhood dreams. Had that really just happened? Back down on the pitch, he walked around in a delighted daze, wearing the white, blue and yellow Canary Islands flag around his neck. The Magician of Arguineguín was now a European Champion.

CHAPTER 13

VALENCIA'S MVP

After an excellent Euro 2008, David was a wanted man. Europe's biggest clubs tried their best to sign him over the summer, but Valencia kept saying no.

'We won't sell David Silva and David Villa for less than £135 million!' the club announced firmly.

£135 million? You could buy a whole team of talented footballers for that money! No-one was prepared to pay the fee, so Valencia's star players were going nowhere.

'Never mind,' David Silva thought to himself. He was still only twenty-three and he wasn't the type of person who got angry and asked for a transfer. Instead, he just got on with his job. He wanted to win lots more trophies, and hopefully he could do that at Valencia.

Unfortunately, however, David didn't play for months because of a bad ankle injury. It was so frustrating to sit and watch and wait. In the end, his season only really started in January!

'Right, I'm ready to make up for lost time,' he told Juan ahead of their match against Atlético Madrid.

David was desperate to get back to his best as soon as possible. As Miguel dribbled down the right wing, he sprinted through the middle, calling out for the ball.

'I'm here! Pass it!'

David's first touch was a little rusty, but he still managed to poke the ball past the keeper.

Goooooooooooooooooooooooooooaaaaaaaaaaaaaa aaaaaaaaaaaallllllllllllllllllllllllll!!!!!!!!!!!!!!!!!!!!!!!

It felt so good to be back! David stood in front of the Valencia fans and blew kisses to them all.

By the second-half, David's first touch was as dazzling as normal again. He controlled Joaquín's

pass and fired a spectacular long-range shot right
into the top corner.

Goooooooooooooooooooooooooooaaaaaaaaaaaaaaa
aaaaaaaaaaallllllllllllllllllllllllllllll!!!!!!!!!!!!!!!!!!!!!!!!

'Man, we really missed you and your magic!' David
Villa shouted, jumping on his strike partner's back.

David Silva certainly wasn't tiptoeing his way
back into action. He didn't have time for that. He set
up goals against Almería, then Málaga, then Getafe
and then Sporting Gijón, and he still had his two
favourites opponents to come.

Barcelona and Real Madrid. They were two of the
many clubs that had tried to buy him after Euro 2008,
but they hadn't tried hard enough. Maybe he needed
to remind them what a big-game player he was...

Against Barcelona, David curled in a dangerous
corner and Hedwiges Maduro bundled it in. *1–1!*

And against Real Madrid, David skipped between
three defenders and then squeezed a shot past his
Spanish teammate, Iker. *2–0!*

Goooooooooooooooooooooooaaaaaaaaaaaaaaaaaaaa
aaaaallllllllllllllllllllllllllllllllllllllll!!!!!!!!!!!!!!!!!!!!!!!!

The Valencia fans cheered and cheered for their little magician. When they needed a hero, they knew that they could rely on David.

'If only I hadn't got injured,' he discussed with Ranzel during the summer. 'That could have been my best season yet!'

David was soon a wanted man once more. Valencia had big debts to pay and it looked like they might have to sell their best players.

'We'll give you a great offer for Silva!' Liverpool announced. They seemed to be leading the long race to sign him because Eduardo Macià, the man who had first scouted David for Valencia, was now working there.

'So will we!' said Juventus.

'And so will we!' said Real Madrid.

'And so will we!' said Chelsea.

'And so will we!' said Manchester United.

Wow, David had some serious thinking to do. Did he want to stay in Spain, or set off on a new European adventure? On the one hand, he loved La Liga and he could picture himself starring in the Real

Madrid midfield. But on the other hand, playing in the Premier League was an exciting idea.

In the end, David's big decision would have to wait another year. Valencia still refused to sell, and so their star players were going nowhere.

'Never mind,' David thought to himself. He was happy where he was, and he would always be grateful to his first club and their amazing fans. He just got on with doing his job again. He was David Silva, Valencia's MVP – their Most Valuable Player.

He stole the show against Villarreal by scoring one goal and setting up two more.

'Magic!' their hat-trick hero David Villa cried out, lifting him high into the air. 'Honestly, what would I do without you?'

David Silva got a hat-trick of his own against Werder Bremen in the Europa League; a hat-trick of assists!

He flicked a cheeky pass through to David Villa. *1–0!*

He chipped a beautiful ball over the top for Juan to chase. *2–0!*

He fooled the Bremen right-back with a lovely Cruyff turn and then picked out his usual target in the box. He always seemed to know where David Villa would be. *3–1!*

'Sorry, I've run out of nice things to say to you!' the Valencia striker joked.

David Silva was enjoying his best season ever. He could now go wherever he liked on the pitch and he was really making the most of that freedom. He was so clever that he could spot even the smallest gaps in the opposition's defence. That was all he needed to create a moment of magic.

Pass, GOAL!

Cross, GOAL!

Shot, GOAL!

With the ball at his lovely left foot, he was simply unstoppable. David finished with ten goals, eleven assists, but sadly, zero trophies. That wasn't good enough for a world-class playmaker like him.

It was finally time for David to leave Valencia and find a big club that really wanted him. But which club would that be?

CHAPTER 14

WORLD CUP 2010

David's club decision would have to wait, however. First, he was off to South Africa to play for his country at the 2010 World Cup. Could he help Spain to win back-to-back tournaments?

'YEAH!' David cheered confidently.

Why not? The stars of Spain's Euro 2008-winning squad were still together, and it was time for them to take home another trophy. First, Champions of Europe; then, Champions of the World!

The only man missing was their manager. It was a sad day for David when they said their goodbyes.

'Thanks for believing in me!' he told Aragonés. 'I owe you everything.'

Then David began to worry, thinking, 'What if the new manager doesn't want me in the team?'

Thankfully, however, the new boss was a big fan of his too. Vicente del Bosque had been the Real Madrid manager back when David had his trial at the club. That was now ten years ago but he still hadn't forgotten 'The Magician of Arguineguín'.

'At last, we get to work together!' Del Bosque said with a big smile.

Phew! David was so relieved to hear that he was part of the new manager's plans. In World Cup qualification, he got three goals and three assists as Spain won ten games out of ten.

'South Africa, here we come!'

David couldn't get comfortable, though, because the Spanish squad was getting stronger and stronger. In midfield, they now had Sergio Busquets, Javi Martínez and his Valencia teammate Juan all trying to force their way into the team. No-one was safe; not even Xavi and Andrés, and especially not David.

'It's a good thing that I like pressure, isn't it?' he joked with his brother Nando on the phone.

For Spain's opening match against Switzerland,
Del Bosque played David Villa as a lone striker, with
five in midfield: Sergio, Xavi, Xabi Alonso, Andrés…
and David Silva.

Phew, he was in the team! Now, it was time for
him to shine brightly enough to stay there. Playing
in his favourite role, David had the freedom of the
pitch. One minute, he was on the left wing and
the next, he was in the middle. He floated around,
looking for that little bit of space between the
opposition defence and midfield. That little bit of
space he needed to create a moment of magic.

'Over here!' he kept calling eagerly for the ball.

Spain passed and passed and passed, but they
couldn't find a way through. David knew that he had
to do something special and soon. He played a clever
ball over the top to Andrés, but he was fouled, and
Gerard Piqué wasted the free kick.

'Stay patient out there,' Del Bosque told his players
at half-time. 'Don't panic – the chances will come!'

Unfortunately, the next chance fell to Switzerland
instead. *GOAL – 1– 0!*

The Spanish players just stood around the pitch in shock. How had they let that happen? And what were they going to do about it? After sixty minutes, the manager decided to make changes: Jesús Navas was on, and David was off.

'Well, that was rubbish!' he thought to himself as he slumped down on the bench.

Uh oh, Spain were off to a terrible start at the 2010 World Cup. And for David, it was about to get even worse. When Del Bosque named his team for the second match against Honduras, he had been replaced by Fernando. Oh dear, did his manager not trust him like Aragonés had?

'I'm sorry, but we've got to have another goalscorer in the team,' Del Bosque explained. 'If we need more creativity, you'll come on, I promise!'

Being dropped was a horrible feeling but David tried not to let his disappointment show. He was a professional and he was proud to represent his country, whether he was in the starting line-up or on the bench. Besides, there was no shame in being second-choice behind midfield maestros like Xavi and Andrés. They were the best in the world.

'Good luck, guys!' David cheered in the dressing room.

He watched and waited as Spain beat Honduras, then Chile, and then Cristiano Ronaldo's Portugal too. David didn't play a single minute of any match. Were his teammates missing him at all? It didn't seem so. His Valencia strike partner David Villa was doing just fine without him. He had scored four goals in four games, including the winner against Portugal.

'You're on fire, mate!' David congratulated his teammate kindly.

He never gave up hope and he never stopped supporting Spain. When David Villa scored another winner against Paraguay, he raced down the touchline to join in the celebrations.

Vamos España!

Winning was a big squad effort, especially when it came to a World Cup. If his nation needed him, David would be ready, and he wouldn't let them down.

With ten minutes to go in the semi-final against

Germany, Spain were 1–0 up. They just needed to hold on and stick together. Del Bosque looked behind him at his bench, looking for someone he could rely on…a-ha, David! 'Get warmed up. You're coming on.'

David ran and ran for the team, right up until the final whistle. Then he threw his arms up triumphantly and cried out,

'We're in the World Cup Final!'

But would he get to play any part in Spain's biggest game? With Xavi and Andrés running the show, they didn't really need another little magician.

In the sixtieth minute, Del Bosque took off Pedro and brought on Jesús.

In the eighty-seventh minute, he took off Xabi and brought on Cesc.

That left one final substitution. David couldn't help getting his hopes up. The score was still 0–0 in extra-time and he was sure that he could make a difference. He could be Spain's hero!

In the on hundred and sixth minute, Del Bosque took off David Villa and brought on…Fernando.

'Oh well,' David sighed heavily. Inside, his heart sank, but he hid the hurt well. What mattered most was Spain winning the World Cup.

And they did it! Just when it looked like the final would go to penalties, Cesc passed to Andrés and he fired a shot past the keeper. *1–0, at last!*

'Yes, yes, YES!' David screamed as he sprinted over to the corner flag for the big squad hug.

It was a second huge success for Spain in the space of four years. First, Champions of Europe; now, Champions of the World!

Campeones, Campeones, Olé! Olé! Olé!

David didn't feel quite as excited as he had at Euro 2008, but he was still delighted to be a World Cup Winner. On the plane back to Spain, he carried his medal carefully in his pocket just to make sure he didn't lose it.

2010 World Cup? Won! Now, it was transfer time.

CHAPTER 15

MOVING TO MANCHESTER CITY

Lots of clubs had been chasing David for years, but few for as many years as Manchester City. They refused to give up on their top transfer target.

It had all started back in the summer of 2007, when City played against Valencia in the Thomas Cook Trophy. The Spanish team had won, and who had scored the winner that day? David, of course!

'Wow, that kid is going to be a star,' the City coaches predicted. 'We should sign him straight away!'

That was easier said than done, however. City tried their best, but Valencia said no. A year later, they tried again, but by then David's value had risen dramatically.

'£135 million for Silva and Villa?' the City owners repeated in disbelief. 'I know we're rich but that's way too much!'

In Summer 2009, Valencia still wouldn't sell David for any less, but by 2010, they no longer had a choice. The club needed money and quickly.

'Okay, we're going to have to let you leave,' they told their star player, 'but only if the price is right.'

David listened to offers from all over Europe. Did he want to stay in Spain and move to Real Madrid?

'No, I think it's time for a new adventure,' he decided.

In the end, David chose to go to England, after speaking to his Spain teammates Fernando and Pepe Reina about life in the Premier League.

'It's the place to be!' they both agreed enthusiastically. 'You'll love it there, little man!'

David had made up his mind, but he didn't go to the Premier League Champions, Chelsea.

Nor the runners-up, Manchester United,

Nor the third-placed team, Arsenal…

No, David chose to move to Manchester City, the team who had just finished fifth.

'Silva's going to City?' some English football fans sounded surprised. 'They're not even playing in the Champions League next season!'

What David liked most about Manchester City, however, was their ambition. Sure, right now they were only in the Europa League, but the club had really big plans for the future.

'We're building a team of superstars that will win the Premier League title in the next few years,' the manager, Roberto Mancini, told David confidently. 'And we think you could be a key part of that project.'

Mancini called him many times during the World Cup to tell him more about his vision for the football club. The more they talked, the more excited David grew. Wherever he went, he wanted to be wanted, and City certainly wanted him.

Their Spanish scout had even visited David's house in Valencia, just so that City could find the right home in Manchester to help him settle in.

'Right, let's do this!' David told his agent eventually.

Unfortunately, Valencia didn't get anywhere near the £135 million they wanted for their two star players. In fact, they didn't even get half of it. David Villa went to Barcelona for £35 million, and David Silva went Manchester for £25 million. City had themselves an absolute bargain.

'David Silva is one of the best midfielders in Europe,' Mancini told the media happily, 'and I hope he will be a very important player for this club.'

Even on day one, David was already talking about his targets. 'I want to bring success to City and win trophies for them,' he told his translator in Spanish.

Holding his sky-blue '21 SILVA' shirt, David joined City's three other exciting new signings: left-back Aleksandar Kolarov, centre-back Jérôme Boateng, and midfielder Yaya Touré. David had played against Yaya in many Valencia vs Barcelona matches. What a difficult and dangerous opponent! He couldn't wait to play alongside him at City.

'I brought these guys in because of their power

and size,' Mancini explained to the press but then he realised his mistake. He laughed and put his arm around his little magician. 'Well, maybe not David here, but he's a fantastic footballer!'

That was the reason why the City manager had signed him; to add something different to the team. Something special.

Before the season started, David got settled into his new home in Manchester. Yes, the weather was a lot wetter and colder than in Arguineguín, but at least he could live a nice, quiet life again. Whenever he had tried to walk around in Valencia, people stopped and talked to him and asked to take photos. But here, he was just another normal human being.

'I love it!' he laughed when Ranzel and Nando came to visit.

Until his English improved, David would have to rely on his family and his Spanish-speaking teammates: Yaya, Carlos Tevez and Pablo Zabaleta. He had played against Pablo at the Under-20 World Cup, Spain vs Argentina, but that wasn't a match that David wanted to talk about.

'Just don't mention it, okay?' he joked.

'Oh, you mean that wondergoal I scored against you?' Pablo teased him. 'Sure, I won't say a word!'

On the opening day of the new season, City's new-look team was raring to go, away at Tottenham. Aleksandar was at left-back, Yaya was in defensive midfield, and David had the playmaker role. He would be sitting just behind Carlos, like he used to do with David Villa at Valencia. Perfect!

David's Premier League debut, however, was far from perfect. The battle raged in the middle of the pitch, and for the first thirty minutes, he barely touched the ball. Then, when he did, *Whoosh!* he had huge defenders towering over him straight away, snapping at his ankles. *Crunch!*

'Welcome to the Premier League!' Carlos smirked as he helped David back to his feet.

'Quick passes!' his teammate, Gareth Barry, called out.

Fernando and Pepe had warned David about the pace and power of English football, but he still wasn't prepared for it. He would need to get up to speed as soon as possible.

David did get into the game in the second-half but he couldn't create a match-winning moment of magic. It finished Tottenham 0 Manchester City 0.

'Hey, you played well,' Mancini told him as he trudged off the pitch. 'Don't worry, you'll get used to this league in no time.'

This was David's biggest challenge yet. He had moved to a new country, with a new culture, a new language and a new style of football. And already, some people were saying that he was too small to be a Premier League star. 'He's going to get kicked to pieces!' they predicted.

They didn't know it yet, but City's little magician was a lot tougher than he looked.

'I'll just have to show them what I'm made of!' David thought determinedly.

CHAPTER 16

TOUGH ENOUGH

A few weeks later, City were drawing 0–0 at Blackpool, with only twenty-five minutes to go. Mancini needed a matchwinner and so he turned to David, who was sitting on the bench.

'Go out there and create some magic!'

'Yes, boss!'

It only took two minutes for David to change the game completely. He set up Carlos with a lovely low cross. *1–0!*

'Thanks, mate!' Carlos cried out as they celebrated together.

That was the confidence boost that David needed. It showed that his hard work in training was really paying off. Now, it was time to become a City star.

James Milner played a quick free kick to David on the edge of the Blackpool box. There were a lot of orange shirts in his way, but he was determined to score his first Premier League goal. He would just have to dance his way through. He faked to shoot and fooled the first defender, then skipped past a sliding tackle. *Olé! Olé!*

'Shoot! Shoot!' the City fans urged. What a wondergoal it would be!

David shrugged off one last defender and then curled the ball into the far corner of the net.

Gooooooooooooooooooooooooooooaaaaaaaaaaaaaa aaaaaaaaallllllllllllllllllllllllllllllllllllllllll!!!!!!!!!!!!!!!!

It was an absolute beauty, one of the best that he had ever scored. David was usually so calm and composed, but not in that moment. With adrenaline rushing through his body, he took off his shirt and whirled it above his head.

'That was magical!' Carlos cried out as David jumped into his arms.

'I'm going to call you "Merlin" from now on,'

Shaun Wright-Phillips decided, 'because you're the greatest wizard of all!'

City were now in second place, just two points behind Chelsea. Could they challenge for the Premier League title already? With such amazing attackers, anything was possible.

David played a no-look pass through to Carlos, who crossed to Mario Balotelli. *1–0!*

From the halfway line, David chipped a lovely long-ball through to Mario, who scored again. *2–0!*

'You're a genius!' Mario told City's little magician.

Too small to be a Premier League star? No way! David was proving those critics wrong, one perfect pass at a time. He had the talent and he had the toughness too. He won City's Player of the Month award three times in a row: for November, December *and* January. When they beat West Brom 3–0, the newspapers called it 'The David Silva Show'. He was a fans' favourite too, especially after scoring in the Manchester Derby.

Now that he had settled in so well, David turned his attention to trophies. There was no better way to launch City's exciting project. So, which one could they win?

The Premier League title? No, it was too soon for that. By February, they were a long way behind their local rivals, United.

Okay, what about the EFL Cup? No, sadly they were knocked out straight away.

The Europa League? No, Dynamo Kyiv beat them in the Round of 16.

'We'll have to win the FA Cup then!' Carlos declared. It was their last chance.

David was determined. He loved cup competitions. He had won the Euros and the World Cup with Spain, and the Copa del Rey with Valencia. Next up: the FA Cup with City.

In the Third Round, he got the ball in the centre circle, dribbled past one tackle, and then split the Leicester City defence with a beautiful ball to Adam Johnson. *3–1!*

In the Fourth Round against Notts County, he curled in a teasing corner and Patrick Vieira headed home. *1–0!*

In the Fifth Round, Pablo's cross was cleared as far as David. He took one touch to control the ball and then smashed it past the Aston Villa keeper.

Goooooooooooooooooooooooooooooooaaaaaaaaa aaaaaaaaaaaallllllllllllllllllllllllllllllll!!!!!!!!!!!!!!!!!!!

3–0 – game over! Carlos gave him a big hug as they walked back to the halfway line. 'Come on, this trophy is ours!'

David set up Micah Richards's winner against Reading to send them through to the FA Cup semi-finals. They were so close to glory now, but their next opponents would be…Manchester United!

'I can't wait!' Carlos said with an evil grin. He had spent two seasons at United before moving to City.

David couldn't wait either. He thought back to beating Barcelona in the semi-finals of the Copa del Rey. What an amazing night that had been! If he could do it with Valencia, then he could do it with City too. They just had to believe.

United started strongly at Wembley, but David helped get City back into the game with his calm and clever passing. They were creating chances and putting United under lots of pressure...

Gareth closed down Rio Ferdinand, who had to pass the ball back to his goalkeeper, Edwin van der Sar. He kicked it out to John O'Shea, but David was there in a flash, so he had to play it across to Michael Carrick. Carrick tried to pass it on to Paul Scholes, but Yaya stretched out a long leg and stole the ball. He dribbled past Nemanja Vidić and then nutmegged Van der Sar. *1–0!*

'Yeeeeeesss!' David cheered, throwing his arms up in the air. Now, City just had to hold on for another forty minutes...

David had a better idea, however. Instead of defending, he led his team forward on the attack again. As long as they had the ball, United wouldn't be able to score! He passed and dribbled and crossed until the final whistle blew.

'We did it!' David screamed with Carlos and Pablo. 'We're in the FA Cup Final!'

It was a famous victory for City and a sign of how far the team had come. If they could just beat

Stoke in the final, they would win their first trophy together.

'Come on, let's end the season on a high!' Mancini told his players before kick-off.

The sun was shining brightly at Wembley, but would it be a beautiful day for City? David believed so and he was desperate to be their big-game player. He raced around the pitch, getting on the ball as often as he could. He was 'Merlin', the greatest football wizard of all.

Just before half-time, Carlos passed to Mario, and the ball bounced down in front of David's left foot. Surely, he wouldn't get a better chance to score? But when he swung his leg, he kicked his shot straight into the ground and it bounced up over the crossbar.

'Nooooooo!' David groaned with his hands on his head.

What an opportunity wasted! He had to make up for his mistake. In the second-half, David played a neat one-two with Mario inside the Stoke penalty area. Mario slipped as he went to shoot but the ball bounced around the box until it fell to Yaya. *1–0!*

'Yeeeeeesss!' David cheered, throwing his arms up in the air again. This time, they just had to hold on for another twenty minutes…

Soon, it was all over, and City were the 2011 FA Cup Winners! As their captain Carlos raised the cup aloft, he shook it so hard that the lid fell off.

'Hurraaaaaaaaay!' the fans cheered happily. They didn't care about a dropped lid; they had just won their first major trophy in thirty-five long years!

As David looked out at the sea of sky-blue shirts, the smile on his face grew wider and wider. Yes, he had made the right decision by moving to Manchester City. If felt like a massive moment for the club, the start of years of success.

The FA Cup winners got a place in the Europa League, but City said, 'No thanks!' They were on to bigger and better things. After finishing third in the Premier League, David would get another shot at playing in the Champions League.

CHAPTER 17

PREMIER LEAGUE CHAMPIONS!

Sadly, City's first Champions League campaign didn't last very long. They finished third in a really tough group behind Bayern Munich and Napoli.

'One point!' David moaned. 'I can't believe we missed out by one measly point!'

Never mind, though, because City were off to a brilliant start in the Premier League. Their amazing attackers were scoring more goals than ever.

Manchester City 4 Swansea City 0,

Bolton Wanderers 2 Manchester City 3,

Tottenham 1 Manchester City 5...

As well as Carlos and Mario, they also had two new star strikers: Sergio Agüero and Edin Džeko.

And as well as David, they also had a new little magician: Samir Nasri from Arsenal.

David didn't mind having competition for his place in the team. It helped to keep him focused on his task – becoming City's MVP. To do that, he would need to get:

GOALS! He scored a tap-in against Swansea and then a swerving strike against Bolton.

ASSISTS! He set up two for Sergio against Wigan Athletic, then one against Fulham.

'Man, I love playing with you!' the Argentinian cheered.

The more matches David played in the Premier League, the better he became. The games used to feel so fast and frantic, but now it was like he had all the time in the world to pick out his next pass.

City couldn't get carried away, though. It was time for their first big test of the season – the Manchester Derby, away at Old Trafford. A win would really show the rest of the Premier League that City were ready to challenge for the title.

From his very first touch, David was on fire. The

Manchester United midfield had no chance against his quick, dancing feet. He dribbled past Darren Fletcher and Ashley Young and into the penalty area. In the end, it took four United players to stop him.

'Keep going!' Yaya encouraged him. 'They can't cope with your magic!'

David twisted and turned away from Anderson and then passed to James, who crossed to Mario. *GOAL!*

With five minutes to go, City were winning 4–1, but David still wanted a goal of his own. Edin played the pass and he dribbled into the United box. Right, time to shoot. He shaped his body as if he was aiming for the far corner but instead, David threaded it through the keeper's legs. *Nutmeg!*

Gooooooooooooooooooooooooaaaaaaaaaaaaaaaaa aaaaaaalllllllllllllllllllllllllllllllllllllll!!!!!!!!!!!!!!!!!!!!!

On his way to the corner flag, David blew kisses to the fans and pumped his fists. Although it was still early in the season, it felt like a very important victory.

David decided to finish things off in style. When the ball came towards him, he flicked it up with his left foot and then volleyed an unbelievable pass through to Edin. *6 –1 to City!*

'You're the best!' Edin screamed, pointing and running towards his favourite little magician.

It was David's new best moment as a Manchester City player. Now, they just had to keep it up…

Manchester City 3 Wolves 1,

QPR 2 Manchester City 3,

Manchester City 3 Newcastle United 1…

But David saved his best performances for City's biggest matches. He scored the winner against Arsenal and set up goals for Sergio and Yaya against Liverpool. He was up to ten assists already.

'Merlin, what would we do without you?' his teammates wondered.

With three games to go, City were three points behind the league leaders, United. And their next match? The second Manchester Derby of the season!

'This is it, lads,' Mancini reminded his pumped-up players. 'We *have* to win this one!'

United, however, wanted revenge for that 6–1 thrashing. It was a very tense match with hardly any chances for either team. Could David step up and be City's big-game player yet again?

Yes! Just before half-time, he curled a corner-kick right into the danger zone. It caused chaos in the crowded penalty area, but Vincent Kompany leapt highest and headed it in. *1– 0!*

'Vinny, you're a hero!' David jumped for joy.

'And so are you!' the City captain replied.

With only two games to go, City were top of the table! They were going to be two gigantic games, however.

First up: Newcastle away. It was 0–0 after seventy minutes, but eventually, Yaya scored two crucial goals. Now, they only had one game to go!

The Etihad Stadium was a sell-out for City's most important match in years. QPR at home sounded like a nice, straight-forward fixture for the last day of the season, but it wasn't at all. They were still battling to stay in the Premier League and so they were desperate not to lose.

From the very first minute, David was the danger man. He dribbled down the left wing and nearly picked out Samir at the back-post.

'Ohhhhhhhhhh!' the nervous City fans groaned in disappointment.

A few minutes later, David found the space to shoot but his shot was saved.

'Ohhhhhhhhhh!' the nervous City fans groaned again.

But David kept looking for that moment of magic. After a great team move, Carlos laid the ball back for him to strike…but it trickled way wide of the target.

'Rubbish!' David said to himself as he pulled his socks up and carried on.

Finally, City's breakthrough arrived. Pablo passed to David, who passed to Yaya, who passed it back to Pablo. He had continued his run and he blasted the ball past the keeper. *1–0!*

'Yessssssssss!' David screamed, along with all the relieved City fans.

In the second-half, however, QPR fought back strongly. *1–1, 2–1!* Suddenly, City were losing, and up in Sunderland, United were winning. Was their title dream about to end in heartbreak?

'No, no, NO! We can't throw this away!' David thought to himself.

City needed their amazing attackers more than ever. Mancini took off Gareth and Carlos and brought on Edin and Mario. But City also needed David's magic more than ever.

He wasn't giving up. He took corner after corner, hoping that a teammate would head one of them in. Vincent, Edin, Mario, Yaya; they had lots of big guys in the box. At last, Edin got on the end of one of David's curling crosses. *2–2!*

'Come on!' Sergio shouted, grabbing the ball out of the net. It wasn't over yet! City still had two more minutes to find another goal and stop United from winning the title instead…

…As Vincent dribbled out of defence, he had David on his right and Sergio through the middle. He chose Sergio, who slipped it through to Mario, and then kept running into the box for the one-two…

…Sergio got the ball back and skipped past one last sliding tackle. He was slightly off balance as he struck his shot but luckily, he was one of the best finishers that David had ever seen. *GOAL – 3–2!*

What? How? City had pulled off the impossible comeback – they were about to win the Premier League title after all! David and his teammates chased after Sergio and dragged him down on the grass. They were too excited for words. They just lay there in an exhausted, emotional heap. They had done it!

All around them, 45,000 fans were going wild. It was the greatest day of their lives.

City! City! City!

When the final whistle blew, they stormed the pitch to celebrate with their heroes. The scenes were extraordinary. David preferred a nice, quiet life, but this amazing moment deserved a big celebration.

He was still in a daze as he walked down the tunnel. Had City really just won the league? Yes, they had! When David entered the dressing room, everyone was dancing, singing and spraying beer and champagne.

'Merlin, get over here!' Carlos called to him. 'We couldn't have done it without you!'

It was true. With six goal and seventeen assists, David had been one of their stars of the season. 'Coming!'

Soon, it would be time for the proper party to begin, but before that, it was trophy time. As the players waited to return to the pitch, they bounced up and down together, chanting:

Campeones, Campeones, Olé! Olé! Olé!

They were now all wearing special City shirts, with '12 CHAMPIONS' written on the front. One by one, they went up to collect their medals until finally Vincent was ready to step forward and lift the gleaming Premier League trophy...

'Hurraaaaaaaaay!' David cheered along with his band of brothers and their 45,000 supporters. He was really proud to be part of such a successful team. He was so happy that he even put on a silly City hat for the photos!

First, Euro 2008, then the 2010 World Cup, and now the 2012 Premier League. What an incredible career David was having, and there was still plenty more to come.

CHAPTER 18

EURO 2012

David deserved a nice, long holiday after his stunning second season at City. After a few weeks of sun and sea in Arguineguín with his family and friends, he always felt fresh and ready to go again.

But what about Euro 2012? Spain were aiming to win a third major trophy in a row, and they couldn't do it without their little magician.

'Silva is our Messi!' Del Bosque liked to say.

After being dropped at the 2010 World Cup, David had feared that his international days might be over. Since then, however, the manager had changed his mind. David was back with a bang. He played in almost every qualifier for Euro 2012, getting four goals and two assists.

'Mate, we need you!' his old Valencia teammate David Villa told him. 'And I need you! How else am I going to score so many goals?'

Sadly, Villa broke his leg just before the tournament, so suddenly Silva was more important than ever for Spain. David's holiday in Arguineguín would have to wait. He was off to Poland and Ukraine to win Euro 2012.

For the first match against Italy, Del Bosque played his six best midfielders all at the same time: Sergio, Xavi, Xabi, Andrés, Cesc *and* David.

'Don't worry, I'll be the striker,' Cesc announced confidently. 'I'll score the goals!'

That wasn't so easy, however, against the world's deadliest defence: Gianluigi Buffon, Giorgio Chiellini and Leonardo Bonucci. Spain passed and passed and passed but they hardly had a shot in the first half. Then in the second, Italy took the lead. *1– 0!* Uh oh, it felt like déjà vu for David. Was it going to be the 2010 World Cup all over again?

'Come on, we can fight back and win!' Iker shouted from his goal, clapping his gloves together.

David knew that he didn't have much time to turn things around. The manager would be making changes any minute now…

As Andrés passed the ball to him, David had six Italians surrounding him. How could he possibly escape? It was going to take a moment of magic. In a flash, he turned and flicked a perfect pass through to Cesc with the outside of his left foot. *GOAL – 1–1!*

'You're a genius!' Cesc pointed at Spain's little playmaker.

That amazing assist turned out to be David's last touch of the game. As he came off, Del Bosque gave him a big hug.

'I'm not sure even Messi could have played that pass!' he said with a smile.

David was delighted. Euro 2012 was already going better than the 2010 World Cup, and it had only just started. Spain's second match against Ireland was 'The David Silva Show'.

It took four defenders to stop David's daring dribble, and Fernando was there to finish it off. *1–0!*

Just after half-time, the ball bounced down to

David near the penalty spot. Three defenders charged towards him, but he stayed calm. He was a man with a plan. He twisted one way, then the other, and passed it through the last defender's legs into the bottom corner. *2–0!*

Goooooooooooooooooooooooooooooooaaaaaaaaaaaa aaaaaaaaaalllllllllllllllllllllllllllllllllll!!!!!!!!!!!!!!!!!!!

So classy! Euro 2012 was turning out to be David's best tournament yet. He threw his arms up in the air and blew kisses to the crowd.

'You're on fire!' Fernando cheered.

David couldn't stop smiling. He was having so much fun on the football pitch.

He won the ball in midfield and poked a clever pass through to Fernando. *3–0!*

He took a quick corner to set up another goal for Cesc. *4–0!*

What a performance! David was the man of the match for sure and there was no way that Del Bosque could drop him this time. In their final group game, Spain beat Croatia 1–0 to make it through to the Euro quarter-finals.

'Yes, we're going to win the whole thing again!' Cesc said, high-fiving David.

It certainly looked that way because Spain had the best squad of players. Whenever they needed a hero, someone always stepped up. It had been David against Northern Ireland, and it was Xabi against France, and then Iker and Cesc against Portugal in the semi-final shoot-out.

'Hurraaaaaaaaay!' David cried out joyfully as the winning penalty went in.

He had been subbed off in the sixtieth minute, but he raced back onto the pitch to celebrate with his teammates.

'I really thought you'd missed that!' David joked with his arm around Cesc.

'No way!' his friend shook his head and smiled. 'Post-and-in is the perfect pen!'

The Spanish squad danced around the field like one big happy family. They were through to their third tournament final – no big deal! Winning big games felt totally normal to them now.

Spain's opponents in the Euro 2012 Final would

be Italy, the team they had drawn with in their very first match. That day, David had set up Cesc to score the equalising goal. Could they become national heroes again?

'YEAH!' they cheered.

Again, Spain passed and passed and passed the ball, but this time, their plan worked perfectly:

Xabi to Xavi, Xavi to Andrés, Andrés through to Cesc...

David, meanwhile, was making a clever run through the middle, in between Italy's centre-backs, Chiellini and Bonucci. 'I'm here!' he called out.

...Cesc across to David. 1– 0!

Goooooooooooooooooooooooaaaaaaaaaaaaaaaaaaa aaaaaaaaalllllllllllllllllllllllllllllllllll!!!!!!!!!!!!!!!!!!!!!!!!

David had scored the first goal in the Euro 2012 final, and with a header too. Not bad for a little magician who was famous for his left foot! He leapt into the air with his fists clenched. What a moment. Starring for Spain meant so much to him.

'Come on!' he shouted passionately at the cameras.

By the time David came off, they were almost there. Jordi Alba had added a second goal and Spain were minutes away from another victory. Just to make sure, Fernando and Juan came on and scored two more. *4–0!*

First Euro 2008, then the 2010 World Cup, and now Euro 2012; Spain were simply unstoppable! David had played his part in all three successes, but this one was his new favourite. He had started every match, he was named in the Team of the Tournament, and he had even scored in the final.

'What a magnificent footballer you are!' Del Bosque told him.

When Iker lifted the trophy, this time David was there in the middle of the front row, arm-in-arm with Andrés. At Euro 2012, he had well and truly earnt his place amongst Spain's superstars.

CHAPTER 19

PREMIER LEAGUE TITLE NUMBER TWO?

What a wonderful year 2012 was turning out to be! David had already won his first Premier League title with Manchester City and a second Euros with Spain. So, what next for 'The Magician of Arguineguín'? Anything seemed possible.

Real Madrid tried one more time to sign him, but again David said no. Instead, he signed a big new five-year contract at City. He was enjoying life in England and he wasn't ready to return home yet.

'We've got to defend our league title!' he reminded Pablo. 'And then there's the Champions League, the FA Cup, the League Cup...'

Unfortunately, City's only trophy of the 2012–13

season came in their first match, the Community Shield against Chelsea. After that, they kept coming close but not quite close enough.

City finished second in the Premier League, a whopping 11 points behind their local rivals United, and they finished second in the FA Cup too, after losing 1–0 to Wigan Athletic in the final.

'Noooooooo, how did we let that happen?' David stood there asking himself at the final whistle, as the rain poured down at Wembley. 'We're so much better than that!'

He looked around at all the sad, soaked faces – Sergio, Carlos, Edin, Samir, Yaya, Vincent...Their team was way too talented to fail. What about the Champions League and the League Cup? No, City had been knocked out in the first round of both competitions.

Although it was very disappointing, there was no need to despair. 'We've just got to come back stronger next year,' David discussed with Sergio.

There were lots of changes at City during the summer, however. Carlos was sold to Juventus, and he was replaced by two of David's international teammates, Jesús Navas and Álvaro Negredo.

'*Bienvenido!*' he welcomed them in Spanish.

There was a new man in charge too. Manuel Pellegrini had been the Villarreal manager during David's time at Valencia, and now the Chilean would be his boss at City.

'I just want you to keep doing what you always do,' Pellegrini told him. 'With you on the left and Jesús on the right, the strikers are going to feel like they've struck gold!'

David crossed to Álvaro. *GOAL!*

Jesús crossed to Samir. *GOAL!*

David played a killer pass to set up Sergio. *GOAL!*

Jesús played a killer pass to set up Edin. *GOAL!*

David slipped the ball through to Jesús. *GOAL!*

'*VAMOS!*' the two Spaniards cheered together.

By January, City were up in second place, challenging Liverpool and Chelsea for the Premier League title.

And by March, they had won their first trophy of the season. David had completed his English hat-trick: the FA Cup, then the Premier League, and now the League Cup too. City smashed Sunderland 3–1 in the final.

'Well done, guys. Now let's go on and do the Double!'

They just had to keep on winning and hope that their title rivals slipped up…

But away at Hull, City were down to ten men after just ten minutes. Uh oh, were they about to lose and wave goodbye to winning the league?

No way! A few minutes later, David passed to Yaya and ran forward into space for the one-two. When he got the ball back, he took one touch to control it and then curled it into the top corner.

Goooooooooooooooooooooooooooaaaaaaaaaaaaaaaaa aaaaaaaalllllllllllllllllllllllllllllllllllll!!!!!!!!!!!!!!!!!!!!!!!

It was only David's fifth goal of the season, and what a brilliant time to score it, just when his team needed it most.

'That was magical!' Pablo shouted, hugging him tightly. '*VAMOS!*'

City had a long, hard seventy-five minutes ahead

of them. David helped out with lots of defending, while also trying to set Edin free on the counter-attack. In the very last minute, he succeeded. *PASS, GOAL – 2– 0!*

'You're the best player in the Premier League, you know that?' Edin screamed, pointing at David. 'We're so lucky to have you!'

David smiled; he was just happy to help his team. With eight games to go, City were one point clear at the top of the table. Now, they just had to hold their nerve...

Manchester City 5 Fulham 0,

United 0 City 3,

'Manchester is blue!' the fans boasted proudly.

Arsenal 1 Manchester City 1,

Manchester City 4 Southampton 1...

So far so good but then, despite David's best efforts, they lost to Liverpool. One disappointing defeat and City slipped down to third place. In the dressing room, Pellegrini's message to his players was clear:

'NO. MORE. MISTAKES!'

Fortunately for them, everyone else was making mistakes too. Chelsea lost at Sunderland, and then Liverpool lost against Chelsea and Crystal Palace. Suddenly, City were two points clear again, with only one game to go: West Ham at home.

As long as they didn't lose, the Premier League title was theirs. But David thought back to their dramatic, last-minute win against QPR two years earlier.

'Let's just win this match and make sure!' he told his teammates.

They always listened to their quiet little magician. Samir scored just before half-time and Vincent scored just after half-time. There would no late drama on this occasion.

'Hurraaaaaaaaay!' David cheered, throwing his arms up in the air. It was time for Premier League Title Number Two.

With a City scarf around his neck, he walked up to collect his winners' medal and then took his place next to Jesús and Pablo on the stage. David didn't feel quite the same excitement second time around, but it was still a very special moment. They had worked so hard all season.

'Hurry up!' they called to their captain, Vincent.

At last, he stepped forward and lifted the trophy. As fireworks filled the sky above the Etihad Stadium, everyone celebrated together – the players, the coaches and the fans.

City! City! City!

Four years earlier, David had made a bold decision to join the fifth-best team in the Premier League.

'Silva's going to City?' some English football fans had sounded surprised. 'Why?'

Well, look at them now – they had won everything! Well, everything except for Europe's top club competition, the Champions League. And David was determined to lift that trophy too.

CHAPTER 20

PEP'S PASS-MASTER

Winning the Champions League was going to
be David's greatest challenge yet. Although City
were improving every year, progress was slow and
frustrating. Twice, they got through the group stage
and twice, they were beaten by Barcelona in the
next round.

'We've still got a lot to learn at this level,' David
admitted to Pablo after another disappointing defeat
at the Nou Camp.

His teammate shrugged. 'Hey, most teams would
struggle against Messi!'

In the 2015–16 season, City won their group
again and this time, they were up against Dynamo

Kyiv instead. That was much better than Barcelona! Suddenly, City were full of confidence and playing their best football.

David's looping corner reached Yaya at the back post. He chested the ball down to Sergio. *1–0!*

Sergio backheeled it to Raheem Sterling, who crossed to David for an easy tap-in. *2–0!*

Goooooooooooooooooooooooooooooooooaaaaaaaaaaaaa aaaaaaaaallllllllllllllllllllllllllllllllllllllll!!!!!!!!!!!!!!!!!!!!!!!!

'Thanks, what a ball!' David cheered as he ran over to Raheem for a high-five and a hug.

Could it be City's year at last? They beat PSG in the quarter-finals to set up a semi-final against… Real Madrid.

'Bring it on!' David said with a cheeky smile. He couldn't wait to take on the team who had rejected him as a boy.

But unfortunately, there would be no big night at the Bernabeu for David. Just before half-time in the home leg, he slid in for a tackle on Gareth Bale and felt a sharp pain in his hamstring.

'Arghhhhhh!' David cried out in agony. He knew

straight away that it was serious. As he hobbled slowly off the field, the fans clapped and chanted his name.

SILVA! SILVA! SILVA!

That turned out to be a game-changing moment. Without their little midfield magician, City stopped passing the ball accurately and creating chances. They looked like a totally different team, and the first leg fizzled out in a 0–0 draw.

'Get well soon, David!' the City supporters cried out in desperation.

They needed him back, but sadly, 'Merlin' had to miss the second leg in Madrid. He watched from the stands as his team lost 1–0 without him. They were out of the Champions League…again.

David liked Pellegrini, but it was time for another change at City. Other than the League Cup, they hadn't won a trophy since the 2014 Premier League title. Having spent so much money, that just wasn't good enough.

The club hoped that a new manager could help to turn things around. In June 2016, they persuaded

Pep Guardiola to take the job. How exciting! At Barcelona, he had led Messi, Xavi and Andrés to fourteen trophies in four years.

'Trust me, the guy's a genius,' Cesc confirmed. 'You'll win everything with Pep!'

Would the new City manager have money to spend? Yes, lots of it! Guardiola made at least one superstar signing in every position.

In goal, Claudio Bravo from Barcelona,

In defence, John Stones from Everton,

In midfield, İlkay Gündoğan from Borussia Dortmund,

And in attack, Leroy Sané from Schalke and Nolito from David's old loan club Celta Vigo.

'Do you think we should be worried?' Pablo asked during pre-season training. 'What if Pep wants to bring in a brand-new team?'

David shook his head. No, there was nothing to worry about. Guardiola liked his teams to play beautiful, passing football and that was his favourite style too. Yes, they were going to get along just fine. David couldn't wait to play the Pep way. What new tactics would he introduce to the team?

For the first match of the new Premier League season, Pep picked David as his captain and gave him a new role to play. He didn't see his little magician as a left-winger or an attacking playmaker anymore.

'I want you in the centre of midfield instead,' the City manager decided, 'where you can control the game for us.'

Fernandinho would be the defensive midfielder, with two pass-masters just in front: David and Kevin De Bruyne. That was a very attacking line-up, but Pep believed in his players.

'Sure!' David agreed eagerly. Less dribbling, more passing; he could definitely do that. Even at the age of thirty, he was still up for improving his skills.

It didn't take City long to settle into their new system. Near the halfway line, David played a quick one-two with Kevin and then burst through the West Ham midfield. On the edge of the penalty area, he slipped a pass through to Nolito, who crossed to Raheem. *1–0!* What a great team goal – that was how to play the Pep way!

On the touchline, their manager clapped and allowed himself a little smile. 'That's it!' he thought to himself.

David was really enjoying his new deeper role for City. He didn't get the glory of so many goals and assists, but now he had more space and time to pick out that perfect forward pass. That made him more of a midfield maestro than ever!

And if they ever lost the ball, he loved the battle to win it back. David wasn't the tallest, but he was definitely one of the bravest. He raced around the pitch with fierce determination.

'Great pressing, David!' Pep applauded him.

After a strong start, however, City struggled to keep it up. They lost to Chelsea, Leicester and Liverpool, and they were even thrashed 4–0 by Everton. They slipped down to fifth place and suddenly, people were questioning Pep's attacking tactics.

'You just can't play like that in the Premier League,' some fans argued. 'When everyone rushes forward, it leaves our defence wide open!'

Pep, however, wasn't going to change his mind that easily. He knew what he wanted to do, so the supporters would just have to be patient. And so would the players. On the training pitch, they practised and practised until every single pass and movement was perfect. David had never played for a manager who cared so much about the tiniest details. It was amazing.

'Nearly!' Guardiola shouted to them. 'Let's try that one more time…'

All that hard work was worth it, though. City bounced back and ended the season in style. David scored the first goal as they destroyed Crystal Palace 5–0, then:

Manchester City 2 Leicester City 1,
Manchester City 3 West Brom 1,
Watford 0 Manchester City 5!

David was becoming more and more important to the team. With his quick feet and silky skills, he made the game look so easy. *DRIBBLE, PASS, PASS, GOAL!* When he played well, City played well. It was as simple as that, and without him, they found it

really hard to win. David was Pep's pass-master and
City's Player of the Season.

'Bring on next year!' he cheered as he celebrated
another great team goal with Sergio. 'We're going to
win the league again!'

CHAPTER 21

CHAMPIONS AGAIN!

'Woah, who's this tough guy?' Sergio joked when he saw David's new shaved head. He looked so different without his shaggy hair. 'Midfielders won't want to mess with you now!'

David smiled; that was the plan. He was all fired up for the new season, and so were his City teammates. It was time to complete their Premier League hat-trick! They thrashed Liverpool 5–0, and they could have scored five more. The fans loved the fantastic football they were playing.

Pass and move, Pass and move, Pass and move...
GOAL!

City! City! City!

'We're looking better than ever!' David argued. A week later, they hit Watford for six.

Kevin whipped in a great free kick for Sergio to head home. *1–0!*

Gabriel Jesus passed to David, who played it across to Sergio. *2–0!*

Sergio slipped the ball through to Gabriel. *3–0!*

David curled in a beautiful cross to Nicolás Otamendi. *4–0!*

Sergio dribbled through the Watford defence for his hat-trick goal. *5–0!*

Raheem won a penalty and took it himself. *6–0!*

What a perfect team performance! The rest of the Premier League had been warned; City were on fire.

Manchester City 5 Crystal Palace 0,

Chelsea 0 Manchester City 1,

Manchester City 7 Stoke City 2...

And Sergio wasn't even playing in that game! City had six different scorers, including David. Leroy crossed to Raheem, who pulled it back to David near the penalty spot. He beat one defender and then poked a shot past the keeper.

*Goooooooooooooooooooooooooooooaaaaaaaaaaaaa
aaaaaaaaaaaalllllllllllllllllllllllllll!!!!!!!!!!!!!!!!!!!!!!!!*

'Finally!' David laughed with Raheem. 'I've been missing out on all the fun!'

The big question was – could anyone stop City? Not when David and Kevin were creating so much magic in midfield. They could pass the ball through any defence!

While Vincent was still struggling with injuries, David was Pep's captain on the pitch. He wasn't a loud leader, but he inspired the other players with his calm determination to win no matter what.

City were drawing 1–1 against West Ham with ten minutes to go. The more chances Leroy, Sergio and Gabriel missed, the more they began to panic. But not David. He pushed further forward, hoping to be the hero…

As Kevin looked up to deliver the cross, David darted cleverly between the centre-backs. The pass was perfect and so was David's stretching left-foot volley.

*Goooooooooooooooooooooooooooooaaaaaaaaaaaaaaa
aaaaaaaalllllllllllllllllllllllllllllllll!!!!!!!!!!!!!!!!!!!!!!!!*

What a touch, what technique, and what timing! The Etihad crowd went wild. When his team needed him most, David had saved the day. City could always count on him.

'You legend!' Sergio screamed as he chased after his teammate.

David liked a nice, quiet life but that day, he had something special to say. With his left arm raised in the air, he put the thumb of his right hand in his mouth. Everyone knew what that meant; he was about to become a father!

'Hurraaaaaaaaay!' the City fans roared their congratulations.

David's celebrations didn't stop there. He scored the opening goal in the Manchester Derby at Old Trafford, and then two more against Swansea City. The first was a fancy flick and the second was a cheeky chip.

'Look at you, showing off your skills all of a sudden!' Raheem laughed.

But unfortunately, there were hard times ahead for David and his family. When baby Mateo was born, he was very ill and so he had to stay in the hospital in Valencia.

'Be there for as long as you want,' Pep reassured his captain on the phone. 'We're all thinking of you and Yessica and Mateo.'

'Thanks, boss.'

Without their leader, City went out and thrashed Tottenham 4–1.

'That win was for you and Mateo,' his teammates messaged him afterwards. 'Keep fighting!'

Everyone was being so supportive, but after missing a few matches, David was desperate to get playing again. He needed something to take his mind off poor little Mateo, and football was his best form of escape. With the ball at his feet, he could forget about his problems for at least ninety minutes.

So, David returned to the City team for the 4–0 win over Bournemouth, but as soon as it was over, he rushed back to the dressing room to check his phone.

'Any news?' his worried teammates asked.

David shook his head and prepared to fly to Valencia again. Those were the longest, most difficult days of his life. David wasn't eating well or sleeping well or training well, but he kept going, for his family and for his team.

'Just take your time,' Guardiola told him. 'Don't worry, sometimes there are more important things in life than football.'

But David was desperate to be back to his best for City's League Cup Final against Arsenal at Wembley. He wasn't going to waste the chance to win another trophy. No way!

It turned out to be a glorious game for three of City's greatest-ever players. Sergio scored the first goal, Vincent scored the second and David scored the third. He turned cleverly past Callum Chambers and fired a fierce shot into the far corner.

Goooooooooooooooooooooooooooooaaaaaaaaaaaaa aaaaaaaaaaaalllllllllllllllllllllllllll!!!!!!!!!!!!!!!!!!!!!!!!

It was game over for Arsenal and a very emotional moment for David. With his left arm raised in the air, he put the thumb of his right hand in his mouth again. Everyone knew what that meant; that goal was for little Mateo.

'SILVA! SILVA! SILVA!' the City fans chanted, and all of his teammates rushed over to hug him, even the subs.

'What a hero!'

'That was magical, mate!'

It was a beautiful moment that meant so much to David. Hopefully, the darkest days were behind him at last. His son was getting stronger and his team was winning trophies. Now, for that third Premier League title…

David burst into the Chelsea box and passed the ball across to Bernardo Silva. *1–0!*

As Raheem dribbled down the right wing against Stoke, David made a striker's run through the middle. When the cross came in, he coolly side-footed it into the net. *1–0!*

Gooooooooooooooooooooooooooooooaaaaaaaaaaaaaa aaaaaaaaaaaalllllllllllllllllllllllllll!!!!!!!!!!!!!!!!!!!!!!!

As David dribbled down the left wing against Everton, Raheem made that same striker's run through the middle. When the cross came in, Raheem couldn't miss. *1–0!*

City cruised to the Premier League title, and they broke lots of records along the way:

The most points in a season – 100!

The most wins in a season – 32!

The most goals in a season – 106!

David was so proud of his team's achievements. At the end of a very difficult year for him and his family, he had won the League and Cup Double! He had so many people to thank for that: the City fans, the City players and, of course, Pep, City's amazing manager. David didn't know what he would have done without their love and support.

Now, everything he did was for his baby son. 'This is for you, Mateo!' David thought to himself as he gave the Premier League trophy another kiss.

CHAPTER 22

ADIÓS, DAVID! HOLÁ, MATEO!

At the end of the 2018 World Cup, David made a big and difficult decision. It was time for him to say goodbye to the Spanish national team. He was very proud of all his international achievements:

125 caps,

35 goals,

'You're fourth on the all-time scoring list!' his cousin Ranzel reminded him.

28 assists,

and, most importantly, 3 major trophies!

And then there were all the amazing memories too, like scoring the first goal in the Euro 2012 final.

'I lived and dreamed with a team that will forever

be remembered,' David wrote in an emotional message on social media.

It had always been an honour and a pleasure to represent his country, but since that Euros success, Spain had slipped up again and again.

The 2014 World Cup in Brazil? Knocked out in the group stage!

The 5–1 thrashing by the Netherlands still haunted David. How humiliating it had been to lose like that with the whole nation watching. They were supposed to be the reigning World Champions! Yes, that was definitely one of his saddest days in a Spain shirt.

Euro 2016 in France? Knocked out in the Round of 16!

David had played in every match, but Spain just didn't look like a trophy-winning team anymore. In the end, Italy had got their revenge for the Euro 2012 final.

And the 2018 World Cup in Russia? Knocked out in the Round of 16 again!

Losing to Russia on penalties had been the biggest disaster of all. Spain were clearly the better team, so how had they failed to win? Well, because everyone was passing, but no-one was moving.

'Make a run!' David felt like screaming in frustration. 'Someone, anyone!'

Now, it was time for Spain's next generation to get a shot at international glory. And at the age of thirty-two, it was time for David to move on and focus on Manchester City and, most of all, Mateo.

His son had spent the first five months of his life in hospital, but now he was getting stronger and stronger. So strong, in fact, that he was finally able to make David's dream come true. For City's first home game of the 2018–19 season against Huddersfield Town, Mateo was there to watch his daddy play his 250th Premier League match.

'I hope you're ready for a magic show, little man!' Gabriel said with a smile.

As the two teams walked out onto the pitch, David carried his son carefully in his arms. Mateo was wearing a City shirt too and the supporters were so happy to finally meet him. They gave him a very warm Etihad welcome.

'Listen to that – they love you even more than me!' David laughed.

Could he make Mateo proud with his performance on the pitch? Of course he could! David entertained him with another midfield masterclass. He was City's pass-master, always pushing the team forward on the attack.

Sergio chipped the keeper. *1–0!*

Gabriel fired a shot into the bottom corner. *2–0!*

The keeper spilled the ball and Sergio pounced. *3–0!*

By half-time, Huddersfield were already waiting for the final whistle to blow. But City wanted more, and David in particular. With Mateo there watching, he needed to create an extra special moment of magic…

As Sergio dribbled towards goal, a defender tripped him up and sent him flying. *Free kick!*

'I've got this,' David told Bernardo and Ilkay confidently.

It was in a great shooting position; twenty-five yards out and near the centre of the pitch. As he waited for the referee's whistle, David stood calmly with his hands on his hips. He knew exactly what he was aiming for – the top-right corner.

David ran up and struck the ball with his lovely left foot. It curled up over the wall…and into that top-right corner! He made it look so easy. The ball hit the back of the net before the Huddersfield keeper had even moved. *4–1!*

Goooooooooooooooooooooooooooaaaaaaaaaaaaaa aaaaaaaaaaaaalllllllllllllllllllllllllllllllllllllllllll!!!!!!!!!!!

David was off, sprinting towards the corner where Mateo and Yessica were sitting. What a beautiful moment for the Silva family!

'That one's for you!' he shouted, pointing up at them.

Then David pulled back his sleeve and kissed the new tattoo on his left arm. It was a picture of his son with two words written underneath: 'Never Surrender'. Even during the most difficult times, little Mateo had never given up, and neither had his dad. Like father like son! David was a fearless fighter too, both on and off the pitch.

'What can I say? He's an outstanding player,' Pep said in his press conference after the game. 'David is one of the best I've ever trained.'

Wow, what a compliment! At Barcelona, Pep had trained Messi and David's former Spain teammates Xavi and Andrés Iniesta. Was he really in that same top category?

Yes! David was too modest to say so, but 'The Magician of Arguineguín' had grown up to become one of the best footballers in the world. With the ball at his feet, he could make the most amazing things happen.

But to make it to the top, you needed to have toughness as well as talent. And David was one of the bravest and most determined players around. Just look at all the trophies he had won: two Euros and one World Cup with Spain, and three Premier League titles with Manchester City.

Now, David just needed to win the Champions League with City and then he and his family could return to a nice, quiet life back home in Arguineguín.

DAVID SILVA
HONOURS

Valencia

🏆 Copa del Rey: 2007–08

Manchester City

🏆 FA Cup: 2010–11

🏆 Premier League: 2011–12, 2013–14, 2017–18

🏆 Football League/EFL Cup: 2013–14, 2015–16, 2017–18, 2018–19

Spain

🏆 UEFA European Under-19 Championship: 2004

🏆 UEFA European Championship: 2008, 2012

🏆 FIFA World Cup: 2010

Individual

🏆 PFA Team of the Year: 2011–12, 2017–18

🏆 Premier League top assist provider: 2011–12

🏆 Manchester City Players' Player of the Year: 2011–12

🏆 UEFA European Championship Team of the Tournament: 2012

🏆 Manchester City Player of the Season: 2016–17

SILVA

21

THE FACTS

NAME: DAVID JOSUÉ JIMÉNEZ SILVA

DATE OF BIRTH: 8 January 1986

AGE: 33

PLACE OF BIRTH: Arguineguín

NATIONALITY: Spanish

BEST FRIEND: David Villa

CURRENT CLUB: Manchester City

POSITION: CM

THE STATS

Height (cm):	**170**
Club appearances:	**615**
Club goals:	**107**
Club trophies:	**9**
International appearances:	**125**
International goals:	**35**
International trophies:	**4**
Ballon d'Ors:	**0**

★ ★ ★ **HERO RATING: 89** ★ ★ ★

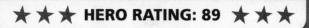

GREATEST MOMENTS

Type and search the web links to see the magic for yourself!

4 APRIL 2007, CHELSEA 1–1 VALENCIA

https://www.youtube.com/watch?v=0dMH8yuByn0
After two successful seasons out on loan, David returned to Valencia ready for his big breakthrough. This was his best moment, in the Champions League quarter-final against Chelsea. David got to the loose ball first, dribbled forward and BANG! His shot curled into the top corner. A new superstar was born.

2 26 JUNE 2008, RUSSIA 0–3 SPAIN

https://www.youtube.com/watch?v=BZZPFftTnzk

This was the night that Luis Aragónes's new-look Spain side made it through to the Euro 2008 Final. It was also David's best game yet for his country. First, he played his part in a great team goal, and then he scored himself after a perfect pass from Cesc. Three days later, Spain beat Germany and David had the first of his three major international trophies.

3 23 OCTOBER 2011, MANCHESTER UNITED 1–6 MANCHESTER CITY

https://www.youtube.com/watch?v=op82rkGfsKY

In 2010, David decided to move to Manchester City to kickstart the club's ambitious new project. This was a massive moment as they thrashed their local rivals at Old Trafford. David was on fire all game long, nutmegging David De Gea and then setting up Edin with one of the best volleyed passes you'll ever see! City went on to win their first-ever Premier League title.

4 | 1 JULY 2012, SPAIN 4–0 ITALY

https://www.youtube.com/watch?v=I6PgcAaMD-4

Spain won their third major tournament in a row by thrashing Italy in the Euro 2012 Final. It was a particularly special moment for David because after being dropped at the 2010 World Cup, he had bounced back to become Spain's little magician again. He was spectacular against Ireland in the group stage and he scored his team's first goal in the final…with a header!

5 | 19 AUGUST 2018, MANCHESTER CITY 6–1 HUDDERSFIELD TOWN

https://www.youtube.com watch?v=MIo31ynqmZ0&t=3s

This might not have been City's most important match, but it mattered a lot to David. With his son Mateo there watching him for the first time, he wanted to create an extra special moment of magic. So, early in the second-half, David curled a beautiful free-kick into the top-right corner. What a glorious goal for City's greatest-ever player!

PLAY LIKE YOUR HEROES

THE DAVID SILVA
TOUCH & TURN

SEE IT HERE **You Tube**

https://www.youtube.com/watch?v=oBDTXozDbzw

STEP 1: Call for the ball in central midfield. You're the pass-master, controlling the game.

STEP 2: Be aware of opponents, but don't worry – you're too good to give the ball away.

STEP 3: Make sure that your first touch is as tight as ever. That ball needs to stay glued to your lovely left-foot at all times.

STEP 4: If you're already in space, ATTACK! Dribble forward, looking for that killer pass.

STEP 5: But if there are opponents everywhere, shield the ball carefully and get ready to...

STEP 6: TURN! All of a sudden, shift the ball to the left, away from any sliding tackles.

STEP 7: Now, you've got the space you need for that moment of magic. *PASS, GOAL!* You're the assist king.

TEST YOUR KNOWLEDGE

1. What was David's first position on the football pitch?

2. Before David, who was the only other famous footballer from Arguineguín?

3. Which former Real Madrid player was David's ultimate football hero?

4. David played for Real Madrid too – true or false?

5. How old was David when he moved to Valencia?

6. Which two Spanish clubs did David play for on loan?

7. Which manager gave David his senior debut for Spain?

8. Who was the other David in Valencia's star strikeforce?

9. Which Manchester City manager signed David in 2010?

10. What role did Pep Guardiola ask David to play when he became City manager?

11. How many goals did David score in major tournaments for Spain?

Answers below. . . No cheating!

HAVE YOU GOT THEM ALL?

FOOTBALL HEROES